This is the book Craig Groeschel was born to write. I felt like I was being let behind the curtain of a life lived at full throttle. Is it a roadmap to getting unstuck? Is it a manual for the kind of life you know you were designed to live? Is it an invitation to an adventure with God? Yes, a thousand times, yes!

—**Jon Acuff**, *New York Times* bestselling author, *Soundtracks: The Surprising Solution to Overthinking*

Craig Groeschel makes change feel possible. It isn't easy to stop what we shouldn't do and start what we should, but Craig serves as a compassionate guide and makes change feel accessible with simple exercises and introspective questions.

—**Jennie Allen**, *New York Times* bestselling author; founder and visionary, IF: Gathering

If you've struggled to change your habits, this book is an immense help. I've read more than a few habit books, but this one made the power to change even clearer and easier to do than ever before. Read this book!

—**Carey Nieuwhof**, bestselling author, *At Your Best*; host, *The Carey Nieuwhof Leadership Podcast*

I often think that when people want to change, they look to remedies and a wide range of self-help solutions. But this book points you to supernatural lasting change by pointing you to the love of our heavenly Father and power in his name. Pastor Craig does it again, writing in such a clear way how change is possible because of God's power in us, not our own.

—**Sadie Robertson Huff**, author; speaker; founder, Live Original

Newton's first law of motion says that an object at rest will stay at rest, and an object in motion will stay in motion unless acted upon by a greater external force. Change will happen only when something greater compels it to happen. In *The Power to Change*, Craig Groeschel provides the blueprint for harnessing the power of biblical truth to change situations we may have long given up on out of hopelessness. This book will truly change your life.

—**Nona Jones**, business executive; speaker; author, *Killing Comparison*

How frustrating it is to want to change some things in our lives and not be able to. Even more frustrating is not knowing why we can't. Here in this book, Pastor Craig brings to light, in a practical and simple way, step by step how to make the changes we want. The best of everything? Based on the power and Word of God.

—**Kaká**, Brazilian soccer player (retired) and
FIFA World Player of the Year 2007

Once again, Craig has put together a deep, practical, and immediately applicable tool for all of us who want to become the people that God sees in us. I can't stop thinking about it.

—**Patrick Lencioni**, bestselling author, *The Five Dysfunctions of a Team*

The Power to Change is your guide to getting unstuck, gaining clarity on your calling, and stepping into the person you were born to be.

—**Jamie Kern Lima**, *New York Times* bestselling
author, *Believe It*; founder, IT Cosmetics

When I read this book, my first thought was "Craig truly gets it!" He sees the importance of how we think, feel, and choose, and how this can impact how we function in our day-to-day lives and our ability to change. His book is a natural outpouring of his genuine love for people and his faith.

—**Dr. Caroline Leaf**, clinical neuroscientist and bestselling author

For the last several decades, Pastor Craig has been such an encouraging voice in helping people become the best version of who God created them to be. In *The Power to Change*, he offers practical advice and biblical wisdom so every person can have great impact.

—**Tim Tebow**, former professional athlete; five-time *New York Times* bestselling author; founder, Tim Tebow Foundation

THE
POWER
TO
CHANGE

THE POWER TO CHANGE

Mastering the Habits That Matter Most

CRAIG GROESCHEL

ZONDERVAN BOOKS

ZONDERVAN BOOKS

The Power to Change
Copyright © 2023 by Craig Groeschel

Requests for information should be addressed to:
Zondervan, *3900 Sparks Dr. SE, Grand Rapids, Michigan 49546*

Zondervan titles may be purchased in bulk for educational, business, fundraising, or sales promotional use. For information, please email SpecialMarkets@Zondervan.com.

ISBN 978-0-310-36718-5 (international trade paper edition)
ISBN 978-0-310-36279-1 (audio)

Library of Congress Cataloging-in-Publication Data

Names: Groeschel, Craig, author.
Title: The power to change : mastering the habits that matter most / Craig Groeschel.
Description: Grand Rapids : Zondervan, 2023. | Summary: "Craig Groeschel knows what it's like to be caught in the dispiriting cycle of trying to change, but failing. This was his story—until he began to discover practical principles for experiencing lasting change in his own life that he has taught to countless others for over twenty-five-plus years at LifeChurch"—Provided by publisher.
Identifiers: LCCN 2022021778 (print) | LCCN 2022021779 (ebook) | ISBN 9780310362777 (hardcover) | ISBN 9780310362784 (ebook)
Subjects: LCSH: Change (Psychology)—Religious aspects—Christianity. | Change—Religious aspects—Christianity. | Habit breaking—Religious aspects—Christianity. | Christian life. | BISAC: RELIGION / Christian Living / Personal Growth | SELF-HELP / Motivational & Inspirational
Classification: LCC BV4599.5.C44 G76 2023 (print) | LCC BV4599.5.C44 (ebook) | DDC 248.4—dc23/eng/20221011
LC record available at https://lccn.loc.gov/2022021778
LC ebook record available at https://lccn.loc.gov/2022021779

Cover design: Stephen Cox
Interior design: Denise Froehlich

Printed in the United States of America

22 23 24 25 26 27 28 29 30 31 32 /LSC/ 15 14 13 12 11 10 9 8 7 6 5 4 3 2 1

Contents

Part 4: Sowing. Not Reaping.

Part 5: God's Power. Not Willpower.

Introduction

Wanting to Change

There are few things in life more frustrating than knowing you need to change, wanting to change, and trying to change, but not actually changing.

How do I know?

Because I have tried so hard so many times to change, only to hit the same brick wall of failure time and time again.

Before I started learning to master the habits I'm sharing with you in this book, that was my life.

One example: Knowing my eating patterns weren't healthy and wanting to do better, I repeatedly tried to change my diet. I made commitments to eat only healthy food. I would succeed all day, but by evening my motivation withered and my willpower weakened.

I would end my successful day of eating right with a little bedtime reward snack of brownies. And something salty. Maybe chips and salsa. And a little ice cream.

The next morning, I'd wake up feeling guilty and do the walk of shame to the kitchen to see the evidence in the sink and in the trash.

Determined to do better, I would eat a healthy breakfast, followed by a nutritious lunch and dinner. But then a bedtime snack of cookies. And chips. And cheesecake.

Finally, I would feel defeated and quit trying. It seemed I had the desire to change, but not the power to change.

You've been there, right?

You've tried to change too. It hasn't worked for you either.

But why?

We want change.

We want to change.

We want life to be different.

We long for more.

Sound familiar?

But honestly, we get tired. Exhausted. Whether physically, mentally, emotionally, spiritually, or all of the above. Change is hard. Trying to change is draining. Our problem is a deficit of power.

Add to the exhaustion our sense of shame because we keep settling for less. We feel frustrated, like I would during my morning-after walks into the kitchen. We begin to despise our desire to change and our apparent inability to do so.

Here are some common behaviors so many of us desire to change. First, there are the "starts." As in, "I'm *going* to":

- Grow in contentment
- Lose twenty pounds
- Feel closer to God
- Breathe new life into my marriage
- Get out of debt
- Be consistent in my Bible reading
- Escape a toxic relationship
- Exercise

Then there are the "stops." As in, "That's it! I am done with":

- Stressing out
- Showing frustration

- Being impatient
- Being late
- Overeating
- Drinking to excess
- Procrastinating
- Thinking negatively

Whether or not I listed any of your starts and stops, you know your problem. You've wanted that "something" to change for years, but you can't seem to find the silver bullet.

If you journal, maybe you've looked back on what you wrote years ago and realized you are still writing the same thing today. Or maybe you've been going to a counselor for quite a while but feel you aren't progressing like you hoped when you began the visits. You're struggling with the same old issues, still hoping for that elusive change to come.

What makes all this so much worse is that you've tried. Like, tried really hard. You haven't just sat around doing nothing. Over the years, you've made a bunch of decisions and commitments and New Year's resolutions and attempts to set goals. Actually, the same decisions and commitments and resolutions and goals. Because, again, you know what needs to change. You have decided to finally do something about the issue—over and over and over. Yet, so far, nothing has worked.

There's a good chance you hate that about yourself. It's embarrassing and creates regret. Each time you try again to change and fail, you feel worse. You look in the mirror and say, "You suck." But you manage to shake it off and go back to your uncomfortably comfortable same old life. Then you get fed up with your problem *again* and decide to change *again*. Eventually, you fail *again*. This time you're not just mad at yourself. You feel ashamed and internalize the failure. Rather than thinking, *I failed at changing*, you think, *I am a failure. I have failed at life.* You have mixed an emotional cocktail of self-hatred and shame.

Here's a question that's hard to hear: What if you're in this same place years from now? Wanting to change but still doing the same things, living the same life?

I know this sounds depressing, but if you haven't seen the transformation you've wanted in recent years, why assume you will in the future? How will something change if nothing changes?

Tragically, this is where many give up. They say to themselves, "I can't change, so I'll stop trying. I guess this is just who I am and how I am."

Does all this mean you're incapable of change?

Does it mean God doesn't answer your prayers?

Does it mean you're trapped with the same annoying problems for the rest of your life?

Not at all.

You can change. I promise. More important, God has promised that change is possible for you. Just as I learned it was for me.

But there's a reason change doesn't come. Scratch that. There are reasons, as in plural, with an *s*.

Bad news: we don't experience lasting change because we try to change in the wrong way.

Good news: we can learn how to change.

Great news: we're going to learn how, together, in this book. We're going to access the power to change by mastering the habits that matter most.

Here's the plan I've laid out for you to accomplish change. Each chapter contains:

- A foundational concept to bring about and build upon change, supported by personal experiences, stories, examples, teaching, and Scripture

- A practical exercise for you to engage with and apply the truths I've given you
- A guiding principle to encourage and inspire you toward change
- A Bible verse from the Father's heart

In part 1 you'll evaluate how you think of yourself, your view of God, and the future you.

In part 2 you'll learn the value of training over just trying harder.

In part 3 you'll discover how hope doesn't change our lives but habits do.

In part 4 you'll see how the reap-sow principle can change the trajectory of your future.

In part 5 you'll grasp how God's power can become the catalyst for lasting change in your life.

For you to master the habits that matter most, I am offering you a clear path to get where you have always wanted to go, the same one I have followed for many years.

If you're ready to start living the life you've been hoping for and dreaming about, let's uncover the first mistake we make in trying to change. Then I'll offer our first solution.

Ready?

To experience change that lasts, focus on who, not do.

Exercise 1

For our first exercise, let's lay some groundwork by personalizing this introduction.

I'm going to ask you to write down the behaviors you want to change. But first, I want you to forget the times you have attempted to initiate a change—any start or stop. To wipe the slate clean, allow yourself some grace and agree to make a new beginning. You may have the same goals, but you'll have a fresh approach. Consider any change you desire, even one you may have given up on a long time ago, and let this be a reset, a refresh, a revival for you.

Write down your "starts"—behaviors you want to change:

Write down your "stops"—behaviors you want to get out of your life:

Finally, if God told you that he would miraculously change one thing in you, right now in this moment, what would you want it to be?

Principle 1

To experience change that lasts, focus on who, not do.

For I am about to do something new.
    See, I have already begun! Do you not see it?
I will make a pathway through the wilderness.
    I will create rivers in the dry wasteland.

—Isaiah 43:19 NLT

Part 1

Who. Not Do.

1.1 Why You Do What You Do

Here's a truth you need to embrace if you're ever going to change: you do what you do because of what you think of you.

Don't confuse this with why you think you do what you do. You may think you make decisions based solely on:

- Weighing the pros and cons
- What makes you happy
- What's best for you and your family

Nope.

You do what you do because of what you think of you.

Let me explain, starting with a story.

Exhibit A: The (Church) Parking Lot Fight

I was a relatively young pastor, our church was still fairly new, and we had just become the proud renters of a small office building. Perhaps we shouldn't have been proud; it was only just big enough to provide space for our staff's offices and for meet-ings. The condition of the building was somewhere between the sets of *The Office* and *Bates Motel*. The neighborhood was, well, questionable. But we'd started our

> **You do what you do because of what you think of you.**

church in a garage and had services in a rented space, and so yes, we were proud to finally have a real office building, even if everything about it was unimpressive.

Until the day we heard, "Fight! Fight!"

Pastor Robert and I were working one weekday afternoon (yes, pastors work on days other than Sunday) when we noticed cars suddenly streaming into our parking lot. Our first thought was maybe it was a surprise pastor-appreciation party. Second thought was there's no way this was a surprise pastor-appreciation party.

The people who were pouring out of a couple dozen cars were all teenagers. Who were making a circle. With two guys in the middle. And those two guys started to take their shirts off.

Ohhhhh. Fight!

Turns out our parking lot was the designated spot for high schoolers to gather off campus when someone said, "We're meeting after school, and it is on!" This was our first fight since we took over the building, and it was about to go down.

I don't remember what I was working on (probably parsing Greek verbs because that's all pastors do on weekdays). I'm not sure what Robert had been doing (probably parsing Greek verbs too). But the idea of getting to watch a fight felt more exciting than whatever we were doing, so we ran out the front door yelling, "Fight! Fight!"

Even though we were pastors, we were still young males, so I'm not going to lie, we wanted to watch the fight. But when we got to the parking lot, we looked at each other and both knew we couldn't. We couldn't watch the fight because of who we were. We were Christians. Pastors. Peacemakers. No matter what we wanted to do, we had to be true to who we were. So we went from, "Fight! Fight!" to, "Break it up! Break it up!"

You do what you do because of what you think of you.

Exhibit B: The Bible

In Proverbs 23:7, God says, "For as he thinks within himself, so he is" (NASB).

What does "for as he thinks within himself" mean? We choose the story we believe.

Two people who have experienced nearly identical circumstances can come to very different self-identities. For instance, if they've been through a lot, the story one might tell herself is, *I'm a victim. Bad things always happen to me.* The other might live with a different identity: *I'm an overcomer. No matter what life throws at me, I kick it in the tail and keep moving forward.*

The Bible says, "For as he thinks within himself, so he is."

What does "so he is" mean? Who we are—our character—shapes our thoughts about ourselves and others. What we think is a reflection of who we are. That then shapes our lives. We have no choice

> **Who we are—our character—shapes our thoughts about ourselves and others. What we think is a reflection of who we are.**

but to live out who we think we are. What we think within ourselves, we are. We make decisions based on our self-identification.

Exhibit C: Psychology

Psychologists and other social scientists have repeatedly confirmed what I experienced in the parking lot and what God told us all those years ago in Proverbs 23—that you do what you do because of what you think of you.

James March, a professor at Stanford University, called this the identity model of decision making.[1] Research shows that, when making a choice, we essentially (and subconsciously) ask ourselves three questions:

1. "Who am I?"
2. "What kind of situation is this?"
3. "What would someone like me do in this situation?"

Your self-identity is a primary reason that you make decisions. For example, if you work more than is healthy, you might:

- Drink two glasses of wine when you come home stressed from work.
- Work out a couple of hours a day but not find time to read your Bible.
- Play video games for hours on end but not find time to work out.
- Yell at your kids for petty things.

You do what you do because of what you think of you.

Often, our identities are an undetected undercurrent pulling us into decisions and behaviors. Sometimes, though, we do sense the current influencing us and then even blame that influence for our poor choices.

Why does your friend keep going from loser boyfriend to loser boyfriend? Ask her. She'll tell you she doesn't want to. It's just who she is. She has always been that way. She wants a guy but always seems to attract the wrong ones.

Why does your other friend always struggle with money? Ask him. He will explain he's just not good with money. He doesn't want to, but he has always spent too much, always been in debt. It's just who he is.

No. That's not the truth about your friends. But if they continue to believe that to be true of them, it will impact their lives as if it were true. Their behavior is being driven not by their true God-given identities but by their self-identities.

You do what you do because of what you think of you.

Exercise 2

Using the "stop" behaviors you listed in exercise 1, think about the belief that is driving your behavior. What is the "what you think of you" motivating the "what you do"?

Get specific in your answers. The deeper you go, the more you can reveal what's in your mind and heart and then the more you can increase your opportunity for change.

Use this exercise to help identify the self-perception that drives your repeated result. Identify the why behind the what. Identify the who behind the do.

When I ("stop" behavior from exercise 1), the underlying belief is that:

Examples:

When I (drink too much), my underlying belief is that (the only effective way to escape my stress and pain is to medicate myself).

When I (choose not to read my Bible), my underlying belief is that (I don't really believe God will fulfill his promises for me).

When I (continue in that toxic relationship), my underlying belief is that (this is all I really deserve).

Duplicate the sentences for each behavior in the blank space provided:

When I:

My underlying belief is that:

Principle 2

You do what you do because of what you think of you.

Jesus looked at them intently and said,
"Humanly speaking, it is impossible. But not with
God. Everything is possible with God."

—Mark 10:27 NLT

1.2 Stagnation through Behavior Modification

- "I'm going to start reading my Bible every day!"
- "I'm going to stop watching so much TV."
- "I am breaking up with my boyfriend—for real this time!"
- "I will not yell at my kids anymore."
- "I'm going to quit smoking."
- "I'm going to stop hitting snooze so I can start getting to work five minutes early instead of five minutes late."

Why do we make these declarations—and then fail to follow through? Could it be we've tried to change what we do and haven't changed what we think of ourselves?

If so, that is a formula for failure. We cannot put do before who, but we do.[2] We do it all the time. We decide to change what we do.

The problem is trying to change our "do" is behavior modification. And behavior modification never works.

Why?

Because behaviors never exist in a vacuum. There's a reason you do what you do. Attacking behavior makes sense because that's what you see and find so frustrating. But if you target the behavior, you are going after the wrong thing.

If you try to change your behavior without changing your identity, you're pulling up a weed without getting to the root.

We've all done that, right? Seen some huge, annoying weed towering over our grass, gone over, and ripped it out with the fury

> If you try to change your behavior without changing your identity, you're pulling up a weed without getting to the root.

of a Marvel villain. It feels great to get rid of the handful of nasty vegetation. Except we didn't get rid of it. Not unless we dug down and got all of the root out of the ground.

To ensure a weed doesn't come back, you have to reach down and pull out what is not visible on the surface.

It's like treating an illness—you can't deal with the symptom and ignore the real problem causing the symptom.

In a similar way, someone who promises to never watch pornography again may avoid looking at it for a few days. But will they get caught up in pornography again? Yes. Why? They dealt with the symptom and ignored the real problem causing them to look at pornography.

Or let's say you decide you're going to get up early and pray every morning. You do, for a couple of weeks, and then you don't. What happened? Did you stop wanting to pray daily? No. Did you decide to end your commitment? No. So why didn't you continue living out the change you wanted? Because you did not reach down deep and pull out the root. You grabbed what you could see, but not the real problem under the surface. You didn't address the reason you weren't praying more.

Motivation and willpower are both limited resources that you will deplete quickly. Behavior modification does not equip you with the power to change.

Are you beginning to see it now? The reason you haven't experienced lasting change is because you've tried to alter what you do and haven't changed what you think of you.

James Clear, a guru on change and the author of *Atomic Habits*, says, "It's hard to change your habits if you never change the underlying belief that led you to your past behavior. You have a new goal and a new plan, but you haven't changed who you are."[3]

Scientists who use cybernetics theory say there are two ways we can try to change.[4] First, there's what they call first-order change, which is behavior modification. We commit to starting or stopping a specific action. First-order change can have some instant results, but the change will never last.

The second approach, according to cybernetics theory, is second-order change, which is conceptual. The focus is not on acting different but on thinking different, especially about yourself. A cybernetics researcher will tell you that second-order change is the only kind that lasts.

Romans 12:1–2 is one of the most popular passages from Paul's letters because the "living sacrifice" reference gets a lot of attention. But in verse 2, the apostle shares the key to transformation—real, lasting, eternal change. "Don't copy the behavior and customs of this world, but let God transform you into a new person by changing the way you think" (NLT). Paul says you'll experience transformation not by changing what you do but "by changing the way you think." *Boom!*

Why would cybernetics theory researchers agree with the apostle Paul? Because you do what you do because of what you think of you.

> To change what you do, you need to first change what you think of you.

So to change what you do, you need to first change what you think of you.

Exercise 3

Taking your "start" and "stop" behaviors from exercise 1, list them again here and then write down the failed ways you have attempted behavior modification.

When you're done, take a look at your list to consider how your efforts were like pulling up the weed without getting to the root. Did you try to treat the symptom while ignoring the real issue? Focus on *doing* without addressing your thinking?

Behaviors: **Modification Attempts:**

Thoughts:

Principle 3

To change what you do, you need to first change what you think of you.

Let God transform you into a new person by changing the way you think.

—**Romans 12:2 NLT**

1.3 True You

My wife, Amy, said that growing up, her friends and even some teachers told her she would always be an average student. She graduated high school with lower grades and continued on that path her first two years of college. That's when I met her.

It was obvious to me that she was extremely bright. I told her so. I wasn't trying to be slick, as in, "I love you because you're pretty, so I'll tell you that you're smart." No, she was truly intelligent. But she insisted she wasn't. I kept proving to her that she was incredibly smart. Finally, my words started to sink in.

Want to guess Amy's GPA her last two years of college? 4.0. Yep. When she changed what she thought of herself, it completely changed how she approached her education, and her high grades were the result. A different and better *who* led to a different and better *do*. Today, she is a respected spiritual leader and thinker, a published author, the founder of a nonprofit for women in recovery, and a mentor to homeschool leaders around the country.

When Amy was growing up, her parents and brother also repeatedly told her, "You're always grumpy in the morning. You're just not a morning person." She believed it. She lived it. Until one day she realized she didn't like starting her day in a bad mood. She questioned why she lived that way. She realized she believed it was who she was because her family told her it was who she was. Amy decided, *Wait. I don't have to believe this. Who says my family is right?* She began to pray, *God, I want to be a morning person. Make me a morning person. I believe I am a morning person!* Ever since she changed her mind, Amy wakes up in a good mood and feels energetic, ready to attack her day.

Did Amy get smart when she met me? Did she become a morning person in one day? No. She was always intelligent, and she always had the potential to be a morning person. Her behavior changed when she finally understood and believed these truths about herself.

Her *who* changed her *do.*

Who you think you are drives your behavior. Since this is true, it's critically important for you to know who you are. Seems easy enough, right? After all, you have never struggled when asked to put your name on a "Hi, I'm ____" tag. You grab that Sharpie and confidently start writing.

> **Who you think you are drives your behavior.**

Still, I wonder whether you really know the true you.

We tend to define ourselves by what we believe influential people in our lives think about us. Psychologists call it the "looking-glass self."[5] We see ourselves through the eyes of others. We let those people define us, but that is not who we are.

You are not what your parent, coach, teacher, grandparent, or the bully at school said you were or made you feel like.

We can also define ourselves by our worst sins or habits. So you might think, *I am fat,* or *I am too skinny,* or *I am an addict,* or *I am lazy,* or *I am a loser.* No. That is not who you are, but we are all tempted to define ourselves by the worst in us.

Why?

One reason is because we have a spiritual enemy. Satan is real, and he is trying to take us out. "Your enemy the devil prowls around like a roaring lion looking for someone to devour" (1 Peter 5:8). The weapon he uses against you is deception. "When he lies, he speaks his native language, for he is a liar and the father of lies" (John 8:44). His primary target is your identity. He knows how essential your self-perception is, so he lies to you about who you are.

That's why:

- After you yell at your kids, you think, *I'm a bad parent.*
- When you don't get the job, you think, *I'm pathetic. I never get any breaks.*
- When you realize you didn't read your Bible or pray again this week, you think, *I'm a bad Christian.*

Your spiritual enemy will repeatedly lie to you about who you are. He says:

- You are a spiritual failure.
- You will never amount to anything.
- You are pathetic.
- You are worthless.
- You will never change.
- You don't have what it takes.
- You can never be healthy.
- You can never be pure.
- You can never have a good marriage.
- You can never be financially free.

But you are not who Satan says you are. In fact, Revelation 12:10 calls him "the accuser of our brothers and sisters." Look at the list you just read

> You are not who Satan says you are. You are who God says you are.

and then think about what he says to you. You've heard some of these false acusations and others.

So who are you?

You are who God says you are. He offers affirmations, not accusations. Because God knew you before you were you. He made you. God knows your worst and your best. The one who knows your worst loves you best. God defines your true you. So who does God say you are? You are:

- Sought after (Isa. 62:12)
- Precious in his sight (Isa. 43:4)
- A new creation in Christ (2 Cor. 5:17)
- Not condemned (Rom. 8:1)
- Forgiven (Col. 1:14)
- Loved (1 John 3:1)
- Accepted (Rom. 15:7)
- A child of God (John 1:12)
- Jesus' friend (John 15:14)
- Free (John 8:36)
- The temple of God (1 Cor. 6:19)
- God's treasured possession (Deut. 7:6)
- Complete in Christ (Col. 2:10 NLT)
- Chosen (Col. 3:12)
- Called (2 Tim. 1:9)
- An ambassador of the Most High God (2 Cor. 5:20)
- God's masterpiece (Eph. 2:10 NLT)
- Able to do all things through Christ, who gives you strength (Phil. 4:13)
- More than a conqueror through Jesus, who loves you (Rom. 8:37)

That is who you are. God said so. You may fear you have screwed everything up, but the depth of your sin is not greater than God's power to forgive. Your bad decisions are not greater than God's power to redeem and restore. When you surrendered your life to Jesus and became a child of God, you didn't just become a better version of yourself, you became *new*.

"This means that anyone who belongs to Christ has become a new person. The old life is gone; a new life has begun!" (2 Cor. 5:17 NLT).

True and lasting change does not come from self-driven, do-your-best behavior modification. You change by God-empowered spiritual transformation, which happens when you embrace your true God-given identity. The statements on the list you just read need to move from words on a page to truths etched on your heart.

Experiencing true change is about not only understanding your identity but also believing it is your identity. If you've believed a lie about yourself for a long time, embracing God's truth about you will not be easy. When you discover what's true about you, I encourage you to pray about it and repeat it. Ask God every day to help you believe the truth about you. And keep telling yourself those truths. If you've told yourself lies for a long time, isn't it time to start hearing the truth, repeatedly?

The list of identity Bible verses is also in the appendix for easy access. Use it to remind yourself of who you are and who God declares you are. Read those truths out loud any and every time you need to hear them. When you accept them in your heart, you'll discover that your old life is gone—and a new future has begun!

─────────────────── **Exercise 4** ───────────────────

In this exercise, let's identify some of the voices that have accused you and told you things about yourself that are not true.

Has someone in your family or some other close relationship consistently told you something that you have come to believe about yourself—even though it is not based in truth? List those lies.

Next, list any accusations you consistently repeat about yourself that are not on your list of lies, whether or not you know their origin.

Which of the identity statements and Bible verses listed in this chapter stood out to you? Write out why you feel that statement and verse (or verses) speak to you.

Principle 4

You are who God says you are.

See what great love the Father has lavished on us, that we should be called children of God! And that is what we are!

—1 John 3:1

1.4 Future You

For a guy whose famous catchphrase is simple: "Alright, alright, alright," Matthew McConaughey spit some truth when he accepted the 2013 Academy Award for Actor in a Leading Role.

McConaughey shared that when he was fifteen, someone asked who his hero was. He answered, "It's me in ten years." When McConaughey turned twenty-five, the same person asked if he was now a hero. McConaughey said, "Not even close! No, no, no.... Because my hero's me at *thirty-five*." The actor explained to the Academy Award audience that his hero is always himself ten years from now, which gives him something to move toward.[6]

I think Mr. Alright, Alright, Alright is on to something.

Hal Hershfield, a psychologist at UCLA, tells us that having a "future self"—a better version of ourselves that we plan on becoming—will change how we live today. His research shows that seeing yourself as a different, future person empowers you to make decisions for the benefit of "Future You."[7] Today, you may want to go back into the breakroom for a second piece of birthday cake—okay, maybe a third—but knowing that's not best for Future You will help you decide to stay at your desk and snack on the bag of carrots you brought from home.

Other research proves that having Future You in mind helps you engage in "deliberate practice." Deliberate practice is strategic learning and growth designed to move you toward a specific goal. Having a Future You target compels you to design your life and make wise decisions to get you there. With no target, deliberate practice is pretty much impossible to engage in consistently. Future You is crucial to lasting change.[8]

Here's an analogy: Let's say I invite you to try your hand at archery. We walk out into a field, you draw your first arrow and place it into your bow, and then you ask, "Craig, where's the target?" I answer, "Target? We don't need no stinkin' target. That's no fun. Just shoot as far as you can out into the field. When we're done, we'll go out and find our arrows and do it again." How many arrows would you shoot? Kind of takes the fun out of archery, right? While this sounds ridiculous, all too often we take this approach to our goals.

In the list of statements and Bible verses in the last chapter, we looked at the liberating truth of who God says you are today. Now you get to dream about the answer to this inspiring question: Who do you want to become?

Who do you want to become?

To encourage you: you *can* become who you want to become.

Many people believe they can't change or won't change; who they are today is who they'll always be. Once again, that is not true.

According to Harvard psychologist Daniel Gilbert, most people recognize they have changed over the past ten years but refuse to believe they can change in the next ten. Gilbert calls this false belief the "end of history illusion."[9] But the data-driven truth is this: you *will* change, and you *can* become who you want to become.

In her book, *Mindset*, Stanford psychologist Carol Dweck writes about people who have a "fixed mindset." Those who falsely believe that who they are today is who they will always be. Dweck explains that unresolved trauma is one reason people get stuck in a fixed mindset.[10] A negative experience can become identity forming.

A son whose dad tells him "You're worthless" for failing an important test can decide, *I* am *worthless,* or *I* am *a failure.* Dweck says the path out is to give beneficial meaning to the trauma. *That happened, but it's not who I am. I actually see the benefit of what happened. It taught me something important and made me stronger.*

Dweck also writes about those who have a "growth mindset," who luxuriate in "the power of yet." People with a growth mindset don't fixate on now because they view themselves as always in a state of becoming. They are confident they are going to become something better, so if they fail or find themselves in an unfavorable circumstance, they view it as a stepping stone to what's next.

If you are afraid you have more of a fixed mindset than a growth mindset, you'll appreciate this: Dweck has discovered, through years of research, that people with fixed mindsets can learn to have growth mindsets.

You *will* change, and you *can* become who you want to become. And it's not only the psychologists saying so; God says so too.

- "And I am certain that God, who began the good work within you, will continue his work until it is finally finished on the day when Christ Jesus returns" (Phil. 1:6 NLT).
- "But God shows undeserved kindness to everyone. That's why he appointed Christ Jesus to choose you to share in his eternal glory. You will suffer for a while, but God will make you complete, steady, strong, and firm" (1 Peter 5:10 CEV).

Guess what? I am writing this on a weekday, so my job as a pastor is to parse Greek verbs. *Told ya.*

The verb translated "continue his work" in the Philippians verse is επιτελεσει. The verbs translated "make you complete" and make you "strong, and firm" in the 1 Peter verse are στηριξει and θεμελιωσει.

I know you might be thinking, *Who cares? It's all Greek to me!* But here's what's cool: all three of those verbs are written in the active voice—meaning the subject, God, is performing the action. All three are written in the future tense, meaning the action will be happening tomorrow and the day after and the day after that. And all three are written in the indicative mood, meaning the action is not something hoped for or wished for but something that will, for sure, happen.

The good work of transformation God began in you—his activity of making you complete, steady, strong, and firm—is something God is doing and will continue to do until his work in you is finally finished.

You *will* change, and you *can* become who you want to become.

So who do you want to become?

> You *will* change, and you *can* become who you want to become.

I want to become someone who is faithful. But I'm always tempted to want to become someone other people think is important. I struggle with wanting others to view me as important for being successful or a good author or the pastor of a thriving church or a popular podcast host.

God did not call me to be important. When I get to heaven, God will not say, "Well done, my good and important servant." No, he didn't call me to be important. He called me to be faithful.

What's interesting is when I aim for the target of faithful, I end up doing what's truly important. Being faithful to my wife is important. Seeking God is important. Handling money faithfully, loving my kids, and being a good friend are all important.

I want to be faithful. That's why my who is all about collecting pens. *Wait . . . what?* I never used to care about pens and couldn't understand why someone would pay a lot for an expensive one. Then in 2006 I received a pen in the mail. Included was a handwritten note from a pastor I had never met, thanking me for and celebrating my "year of faithfulness" to Jesus and my wife, kids, and church. Turns out this spiritual leader sent pens annually to a long list of pastors he wanted to honor and remind to be faithful.

In 2006 I somehow made the list and received my first pen. I finally met the person sending the pens in 2012. When I asked who else was on his pen list, his expression turned sad as he said, "Unfortunately, the list of people I send them to is smaller than it used to be."

We shared a knowing look, thinking about the tragic stories of spiritual leaders who burned out or made sinful decisions and no longer met the standard to receive a pen. That's why receiving a pen represents who I want to become. It's not about the pen but about the position in which God has placed me. I want to be someone who is faithful to Jesus, my family, and my church—all the way to the end.

That's me. Who do *you* want to become?

A true man of God?
A better husband and father?
A godly woman?
A better wife and mom?
A bold witness for Jesus?
A person who is sober and living free of self-destructive habits?
A radically generous giver?
A person who is healthy?

Whoever you want to become, you *can* become that person. And knowing that you are called to more, who you truly are—and who you want to become—is how you begin any successful attempt at change.

Are you ready to finally see that happen?
Well, alright, alright, alright!

Exercise 5

Take a few minutes to write about Future You—the hero you'll be in ten years. Create a target for yourself. Engage in deliberate practice. Tell yourself and God who you want to become. When you're done, pray and commit this new vision to him and ask for his help.

Principle 5

**You *will* change, and you *can* become
who you want to become.**

For I can do everything through Christ, who
gives me strength.

—Philippians 4:13 NLT

1.5 Called to Who (Before Do)

Do you ever feel called to more?

We live in a culture of more—more promotions, money, square feet, clothes, vacations, followers. But have you noticed how even when you get more, you just want more?

Why?

Because that brand of more comes from our sin. While one of the many downsides of our fallen nature is to never be satisfied for long with what we have, God made us for a far more significant kind of more.

If you have ever felt called to more, it's because you *are* called to more. But the right kind of more. God uniquely created you, gave you gifts, set you apart, and called you: "Therefore I, a prisoner for serving the Lord, beg you to lead a life worthy of your calling, for you have been called by God" (Eph. 4:1 NLT).

When most Christians hear that they are called, they tend to think about do, not who. They

> If you have ever felt called to more, it's because you *are* called to more.

wonder what task, ministry, or job God might be calling them to. Or if God has a specific place for them to live. Some worry they might even miss their calling.

A calling is one way to discover our do. But we learn in the Bible that, as with our attempts to change, a calling focuses on who before do.

In Genesis 12:1, God tells Abram, "Go from your country, your people and your father's household to the land I will show you." Verse 4 states, "So Abram went, as the LORD had told him." There was no do yet, only who!

In the Ephesians 4 verse, Paul says you have been called to what? A life. "You have been called," so you should "lead a life worthy of your calling." And check out 2 Timothy 1:9: "For God saved us and called us to live a holy life" (NLT).

You are called not just to a life but to a holy life.

Yes, you are also called to a ministry, to a do, but that is secondary. Who comes before do. God has called you to a holy life, to be faithful to him, to realize nothing else compares to "the surpassing worth of knowing Christ Jesus" (Phil. 3:8) and so to live, first and foremost, for Jesus.

"And whatever you do, whether in word or deed, do it all in the name of the Lord Jesus, giving thanks to God the Father through him" (Col. 3:17).

What God would have us do and where God would have us go is secondary. Whatever God has you do, you do that for Jesus. Wherever God puts you, you serve Jesus. *That's* your calling.

Your calling is more about who you are becoming than what you are doing. Let me repeat—your calling is more about who you are becoming than what you are doing. You are called not only to serve Jesus but also to become more and more like him. The more is discovered in the becoming.

Another way to say this is you are called first to salvation, then to sanctification, then to serving. Sanctification and serving will then run parallel until heaven. The two work hand in hand.

Here's what that looked like for me: In college, I was an absolute mess and as far from God as you can imagine. Then my fraternity got in a lot of trouble. Mostly as a public relations move at first, I decided to start a Bible study.

I began to read the Bible, specifically the Gospels. As I read, I felt drawn to Jesus, so I kept reading. Finally getting to Paul's letters, I came to a verse in Ephesians that says you are saved by grace, not by works. That spoke to me because I knew I could never be good enough for God. I felt him inviting me to put my faith in Jesus, and I did. God called me to salvation. I responded.

I was now a Christian, but I had no idea what that really meant. True story: I had a fraternity brother in my fraternity who, unrelated to me, also became a Christian. We decided to celebrate by going out and getting drunk. We just didn't know any better yet.

I was a Christian, but I was nothing like Christ. Gradually, I came to know Jesus more and what it meant for me to live like him. With God's help, I started to not only identify sin but also say no to it.

As I grew in maturity, I would take several steps forward and then a couple back. That ongoing process, which is still happening today, of letting God's Word, empowered by God's Spirit, conform me to the image of Christ was God's calling to sanctification. I was responding.

Before long, I realized I was also called to serve. In fact, after experiencing salvation and beginning to be transformed through God's sanctification process, I felt compelled to serve. I felt him calling me to become a pastor. It made no sense to me or to anyone else—as confusing as John Wick becoming a monk or a mongrel becoming a poodle—but his call was undeniable. I knew I had to answer.

Your call to serve will look different from mine. You might volunteer with teenagers, start a ministry, sing in a worship band, edit videos, or teach kids, but the process will be the same. God will call you to salvation, then sanctification, then service. Why? Because who comes before do.

Serving is about what you were gifted by God to do and through which ministry you should do it. But before do comes the who of salvation. We first put our faith in the right who, Jesus, because "salvation is found in no one else, for there is no other name under heaven given to mankind by which we must be saved" (Acts 4:12).

After putting your faith in the right who for salvation, your next priority is becoming the right who through sanctification. Sanctification is God's process of freeing you from sin and making you holy so you might "be conformed to the image of his Son" (Rom. 8:29), who is "your example, and you must follow in his steps" (1 Peter 2:21 NLT).

Prioritize putting your faith in Jesus and partnering with God in his sanctifying work of making you more like Jesus. Then you can get into the specifics of what you are supposed to do.

Understanding our who illuminates our do. When you have clarity about the unique way in which God made you, you will start to understand what God has for you to do.

Knowing this, what might be your do? Is there a specific calling you sense God has put on your life?

You might feel led to serve in your church or community in some way that flows out of your unique gifting. Or to start a ministry or nonprofit. Or maybe you've felt a tug toward doing inner-city or overseas missions.

You may discern a calling not to a mission or ministry but to get your marriage or finances right, focus on your child's relationship with Jesus, or establish the habit of praying and reading the Bible every day.

That calling or goal might feel small—especially compared with someone on the verge of moving across the world to become a missionary—but it is not small. Your do is not small if it is connected to your who.

> **Your do is not small if it is connected to your who.**

Let's think about the two whos of Jesus and you and how they give significance to your dos.

If your first who is Jesus—whatever you do, you're doing it for Jesus—then your do is not small.

I think of the time when James and John came to Jesus and asked if, when he came to power, they could have the two biggest positions of authority under him. *Jesus, you're pretty dope. But, well, we're kinda dope too. So we think we should be like, you know, kind of your vice presidents.* Jesus used their request to call all twelve of the disciples to gather for a huddle. He told them, "You know that the rulers in this world lord it over their people, and officials flaunt their authority over those under them. But among you it will be different. Whoever wants to be a leader among you must be your servant, and whoever wants to be first among you must be the slave of everyone else. For even the Son of Man came not to be served but to serve others and to give his life as a ransom for many" (Mark 10:42–45 NLT).

Jesus told them: If you're going to follow me, you're going to have to flip your ideas—of what is big and what is small, of who is important and who is not, of what is first and what is last—upside down. If you want the top leadership positions, you have to choose to be at the bottom. Small is the new big.

There is a great example of this in the next chapter—Mark 11. Jesus and the disciples were approaching Jerusalem. This was a huge moment. In this one week, Jesus would enter Jerusalem; have the last supper with his disciples; pray and get arrested in the garden; go through trials; be tortured, crucified, and buried; and then rise from the dead. *Wow.*

This all started with what we now call the "triumphal entry," when Jesus came riding into town and people laid out palm branches like a red carpet to celebrate his arrival. The disciples felt the significance of this moment. They were the closest to Jesus and had left so much to follow him, so it kind of felt like their moment too.

Then, when they were almost at the town, when it was all about to go down, Jesus chose two of them for a special assignment. *Whaaaa? A special assignment? Yes!* They had to have thought Jesus was revealing who he considered to be the most important disciples. But then he explained the assignment: "Go into the next village. As soon as you enter it, you will find a young donkey that has never been ridden. Untie the donkey and bring it here. If anyone asks why you are doing this, say, 'The Lord needs it and will soon bring it back'" (Mark 11:2–3 CEV).

You can picture the two who were chosen thinking, *W-w-w-wait a minute. Hold up. We got… donkey duty?* A moment ago, they'd had visions of Jesus asking them to cast out demons or call down fire from heaven or boldly proclaim Jesus' arrival. *Not* donkey duty.

Mark does not tell us who Jesus picked, but I want to believe he chose James and John. *So you want the biggest leadership roles? How about you take some donkey duty?*

Jesus gave two of his twelve guys an assignment, and the two were probably disappointed. But the disciples were about to learn that the size of your assignment never determines the significance of your impact. The size of your assignment—the do God is calling you to—may be far more important than it feels or than you can imagine.

Think about those two disciples. They had no idea that donkey duty meant bringing to Jesus what would carry him to his calling. That the donkey would deliver Jesus to his destiny. I bet when the disciples talked months later about the eternal impact of that weekend, everyone was jealous of the two who got to serve Jesus by fetching a donkey for him. Yep, in hindsight, donkey duty became an envied position.

Whatever God might be calling you to do, I know that if Jesus is your first who, your do is not small.

If your do is about who God wants you to become, about who you want to become, then your do is not small.

Here's how this works in a common goal: Let's say you want to lose fifteen pounds. On its own, that may not feel like a goal with much weight. (Pun intended.) But if that goal is driven by your who, it is eternally significant. Why do you want to lose fifteen pounds? "Because of my who—I am the temple of God. I know I can be more true to my who if I am in better shape physically. Also, God has called me to serve, so I want to have as much energy and strength as possible to faithfully serve Jesus and be a part of his mission. Losing fifteen pounds will help me toward that goal."

Whoa. Do you feel the weight of *that?* That goal is not about looking good in a swimsuit this summer or getting back into those favorite jeans. That's about God, about Jesus, about who you're becoming, about the eternal impact you want to have with your life.

If your do is about who God wants you to become and who you want to become, then your do is not small.

You see the power of starting with who? This understanding will help you change in ways you have not been able to change. So let's get super practical and learn how to start with who.

--- **Exercise 6** ---

SALVATION

If you are a follower of Jesus, briefly write out your testimony— how you came to salvation in Christ. (Look back over my story, if needed.)

SANCTIFICATION

List the most significant changes Christ has made in your life since salvation.

SERVING

What is your do—your calling to serve?

Is there a service that you sense God has called you to do, but the opportunity has not come about yet? Explain.

Principle 6

If your do is about who God wants you to become, about who you want to become, then your do is not small.

Whoever is the least among you is the greatest.

—Luke 9:48 NLT

1.6 Start with Who

I have a thing for giving people nicknames. I don't like to brag, but I'm like the Oprah Winfrey of nicknames. "You get a nickname! You get a nickname! Everyone gets a nickname!"

If you work with me long enough, I'll give you a nickname. Hopefully, you'll like it, but if not, sorry. I'm the nickname boss, and yours is probably going to stick.

It's not just coworkers. I call the guy I work out with "Paco." (He also calls me "Paco," which can get a little confusing.)

I call Amy "Bear." (She also calls me "Bear." Also potentially confusing, but love makes it work.)

I have nicknames for all my kids. (I have a lot of kids, so that's a lot of nicknames!) Their birth certificates don't say so, but to me, my children are Catie Cat, Mandino, Anna Banana, Sambo, Bookie, and Jojo.

God has a thing for changing people's names. (Which I have never done. I'll give people who work for me nicknames, but changing their actual names seems above my pay grade.)

According to Genesis 17, God told a guy named Abram (paraphrasing in GCV, the Groeschel Contemporary Version), "Bro, I know you've been rolling with Abram, but from now on your name will be Abraham."

Abram must have looked up to the heavens cross-eyed. "Um, God, not one to argue with you, but Abraham means 'father of many,' and I am father of, uh, none. That's the worst thing in my life. I have no children. So, well, people might laugh if I tell them to call me father of many."

God was like, "Sorry, you're Abraham. I'm changing your wife's name too. No more Sarai. From now on she's Sarah."

"But, God," Abraham stammered, "Sarah means 'princess, mother of nations.' She's the mother of no one."

Keeping with his track record, God won that argument. From that point on, Abram and Sarai were Abraham and Sarah.

The couple ended up having a child, Isaac. Isaac and his wife, Rebekah, had a son they named Jacob. The name Jacob means "supplanter." A supplanter is someone who takes someone else's place. The name referred to when Jacob came out of the womb, grabbing his twin brother's foot as if he were trying to hold him back so Jacob could be born first. Jacob ended up living out that name as he deceived his father to take his older brother's place and blessing. But Genesis 32 says that God renamed Jacob "Israel," which means "one who has wrestled with God."

Later in the Bible, in the book of Judges, we meet Gideon, threshing wheat in a winepress. That's weird. You press grapes in a winepress. Why was Gideon threshing wheat in there? Because he was hiding. He had to do his work but was terrified of his people's enemy, the Midianites.

So Gideon threshed his wheat in a place where no one would see him. That's when an angel showed up and said, "The LORD is with you, mighty warrior" (6:12). Gideon must have thought the angel was talking to someone else, but no, God was calling Gideon a mighty warrior.

Then there was the time when Jesus met this young fisherman named Simon and said, "You are Simon, son of John. You will be called Peter" (John 1:42 GCV). That is not normal. If I met some dude for the first time and he said, "You are Craig, son of Tom. You will be called Barry," I'd be like, "No. You don't get to rename me, and no one is calling me Barry." (No offense if your name is Barry. Work with me, okay?)

But Jesus told Simon his days of being Simon were over and his future was forever as Peter. Peter means "rock." Peter was not a rock. Yet. He was bombastic, up and down, hot and cold, tossed back and forth. But Jesus said, "You are Peter, a rock."

Why did God change those people's names? Because he knew who they truly were, who they would become, and what they needed to do.

- Abram and Sarai were going to have children and become the father and mother of the nation of Israel.
- Jacob's children would become the original twelve tribes of Israel.
- Gideon would become the mighty warrior who led God's people into battle against the Midianites.
- Peter would become a foundation, a stabilizing influence for the early church.

God changed their names because change starts with your identity. You do what you do because of what you think of you. For them to do what they needed to do, they first had to think the right thing about themselves.

For you to do what you need to do, for you to change, you first need to think the right thing about yourself. You need to know your true identity, understand your true identity, and start with your identity. You start with who, not do. Why? Because your identity drives your behavior. If you don't start with your identity, any behavior change you make won't last.

So that's the concept. Now, let's get practical. Let me show

> **If you don't start with your identity, any behavior change you make won't last.**

you how this approach can impact your attempts to change in the future.

For example, let's say you've thought repeatedly, *I am going to stop gossiping all the time*. You've tried. It hasn't worked. Why? Because it's behavior modification. If you make any progress at all with this method, it's not likely to last. You want to start with your identity. So you might decide, *As a follower of Jesus, I'm called to love and speak well of others. Because of who I am in Christ, I will build people up rather than tear them down*. See how that puts who before do?

You and your spouse may have a goal of a better marriage. The first problem with this is it's hard to know if you ever reach your goal, because what exactly is a "better marriage"? But the more significant issue is that this goal does not start with your identities. What might be a better marriage goal? *Because I am a godly husband, I will pray with my wife daily, and we will be part of a couples' small group together, which will help us have a better marriage.*

That starts with who you are and gives you a specific and strategic habit to move toward the change you want. This is absolutely necessary, and we'll learn how to choose and establish that strategy later in the book.

One more example: Let's say you smoke and decide to quit. You're on a break at your job, and a coworker asks, "Want a cig?" What are you likely to say? "No thanks, I'm trying to quit." What does that communicate? "I'm a smoker who is trying to do something else." That change won't last. It's behavior modification, not based on identity transformation.

So what should you say? "No, thanks, I don't smoke." That could lead you to victory. Why? Because it starts with your identity. You've made it about who you are. Regardless of your past behavior, you are saying that you're not a smoker. You are a new creation in Christ. A smoker is never who you truly were, and it's definitely not who you truly are anymore. So you tell your coworker, "No, thanks, I don't smoke," and you tell yourself, *Because my body is the temple of God.*

That's a *who before do* approach to change, and, with God's help, it will work, allowing you to discover the change you've longed for but never experienced.

So who do you want to be?

Think about it. Be specific. If Future You is your hero, what qualities should Future You possess? Who do you want to become? Do you want to be debt free? Irrationally generous? A godly spouse? An involved parent? Healthy in a way that honors God? Pure in mind and heart? Addiction free? Respected? Faithful? A selfless servant?

It's time to change, to become the person God created you to be. God is already doing that in you. He will continue until the job is done. You can partner with him by choosing the change you most need to make now. But to see that change happen, you've got to start with who. Not do.

That's how you start. Next, you're going to need power—the power to change—a power you don't possess. While you don't have the power you need, we'll soon learn that it's both available and accessible.

Exercise 7

Complete this open-ended sentence with true aspects of your life: If today, I lost [blank], I would feel totally lost and not know what to do.

Examples: a job, money, social status, a talent or skill

Describe how each aspect of life you wrote down is connected to who you are—your identity—and not just what you do.

How can you turn each one from do to who? How can you surrender that aspect of your life to the point where, if God took it away, you'd still be okay?

> Example: I feel like my career has become who I am, not just what I do. But if I got let go or could no longer do that work, I would still be a child of God, still have my life, calling, and family. I would still have the most important things in my life.

Principle 7

To change, you need to think the right thing about yourself, know your true identity, and start your identity with who, not do.

I am certain that God, who began the good work within you, will continue his work until it is finally finished on the day when Christ Jesus returns.

—Philippians 1:6 NLT

Part 2

Training. Not Trying.

2.1 The Thing about Goals

It's time to define your win. After all, defining your win *is* how you begin.

So how do you determine your win? How is a goal conceived? While this can happen in all kinds of ways, it often happens when a pain point bubbles to the surface in your life. For an example, I'll share how one of my goals was born.

I have six kids. *That's half a dozen.* An entire starting hockey team. How many geese there were a-laying. A Brady Bunch. A *lot* of kids.

I also have a church I pastor. A staff of hundreds I lead. Books I write. A podcast I produce. Conferences I speak at. Like you, my schedule stays pretty dang busy.

Over the years, my kids would sometimes ask me to do something. I would apologetically say no. I loved spending time with them but felt like I was just too busy. Something on my agenda seemed too pressing. My kids were getting older and my time with them shorter, but I still often felt forced to say no to time together.

> Defining your win is how you begin.

One day, I was reading a book by Chip Heath and Dan Heath called *The Power of Moments: Why Certain Experiences Have Extraordinary Impact.* Their words hit me like a Mike Tyson punch to the throat. I was reading the book for my job, trying to figure out how I could create amazing moments *at church.* But I should have been reading the book for my family. I needed to create amazing moments with my children.

I realized my church can find another pastor. Someone else can do a leadership podcast. (And there are many who do). But my kids will never have another dad. I needed to get better at prioritizing them.

Instantly, I defined a new win: to create moments of extraordinary impact with my kids. I didn't want to miss any more opportunities with them, so I decided:

1. If they initiated, I would say yes and do what they wanted to do for as long as they wanted to do it.
2. I would initiate a meaningful conversation with them daily. (Not necessarily *all* of them every day. I mean, there are six!)
3. I would initiate an activity they love weekly.

I was excited.

I should have been excited and *apprehensive*. I had no idea saying yes would lead to having my fingernails painted or to a bunch of teenage girls doing my hair. I could not have predicted the number of hours I would spend learning TikTok dances or playing pickleball. We also climbed a giant cross. We found our way onto the roof and catwalk of our church. I cannot count how many late-night fast-food and ice-cream runs we have made. None of that fits with the rhythm of how I prefer to do life. I committed to doing what they wanted for as long as they wanted. I did not realize my son Stephen would want to play catch from now until Easter. Of 2029!

Defining and working toward my new win didn't take shape the way I had imagined. It has taken far more time than I expected. Yet I have loved every minute. I had no idea that quality time with my kids would lead to unbelievably great conversations. I never anticipated my son would tell his friends, "My dad is my best friend." *Wow.*

I started by defining my win: to create moments of extraordinary impact with my kids.

Have you defined your win? This step is so vital to creating real change. Defining your win is how you begin.

But spoiler alert: defining the win is not—I repeat not—*how* you win. We will get to that. Defining the win is not how you win but how you begin. You create a goal, and goals are great.

Why? Because goals give you direction.

Goals Give Direction

We are so easily distracted. We can wander down wrong paths without even realizing it. Like how I didn't know what I was missing with my kids until I defined my win.

We need direction because, without it, we are running a race we can't win.

The book of 1 Corinthians is a letter Paul wrote to the Christians in Corinth, a city in Greece. He told them, "Don't you realize that in a race everyone runs, but only one person gets the prize? So run to win!" (9:24 NLT).

Paul gave the example of an athlete who "competes in the games" (v. 25). He wrote this in about 55 AD. The Olympic Games took place in Olympia, Greece (hence the name), every four years from 776 BC to 393 AD. Corinth was also the location of the Isthmian Games. Because of this, the Corinthians would have understood Paul's athletics metaphor. He wrote how, like in a competitive race, only one runner gets the prize. Only one gets the gold.

He challenged them, and us, "Run to win!"

Paul continued, "I don't run without a goal" (v. 26 CEV).

Paul knew the finish line of his race. Earlier in the letter he clearly described his life's purpose—to preach the gospel. That was the one goal that drove Paul. He also said, "However, I consider my life worth nothing to me; my only aim is to finish the race and complete the task the Lord Jesus has given me—the task of testifying to the good news of God's grace" (Acts 20:24).

Paul set a destination and knew exactly where he was going. He had a goal. That goal gave him direction. Paul defined his win.

Not everyone does. It's easy to run without knowing the location of the finish line.

After winning a gold medal in the 1984 Summer Olympics in Los Angeles, Mauro Prosperi decided to compete in the 1994 ultramarathon in Morocco—a *week*long race. Mauro disappeared on the fourth day. He ran into a sandstorm, which caused him to go *181 miles* off course. He had no idea where he was going. He was completely lost but still continued to run—for nine days![11]

Everyone is running, but some are running aimlessly. For them, life feels like a race every day. They feel pressure to win. So they take off. They're running but don't really know where they're going. With no finish line in mind, they're "chasing the wind," as King Solomon describes in Ecclesiastes (2:11 CEV).

Is that you?

God told us, through Paul, "Run to win!" But if you don't know the location of the finish line, how can you?

Here's what tends to happen to people who haven't defined a win: they settle for someone else's.

Your parents may decide what they want for your life. Without your own goal, you'll fall into their plan as if you have no choice.

Bosses most assuredly have a way they want your life to go. They will enforce their will unless you are committed to running your own race.

Most commonly, people without a defined win fall into the

current of culture. They live like everyone else. Not having a finish line makes it easy to want a new car like your neighbor's, a promotion like your coworker's, and a vacation like your friend's. You're living *a* life, but it's not really *your* life.

You are wise to decide where you want your life to go. So what's your finish line? What's your win? Do you know?

I encourage you to set finish lines for the most important areas of your life.

Prayerfully decide what your win is in your:

- Relationship with God
- Ministry
- Marriage
- Parenting
- Relationships with others
- Career
- Finances
- Physical health

You cannot do what you don't define. How can you win if you don't have a finish line?

Don't let this overwhelm you. If you do, you won't change. If you haven't already, choose just one win to focus on as you go through this book, no matter how many things you would love to change or accomplish. Narrow

You cannot do what you don't define.

your goals down to one that you sense is critical right now. You may choose something that feels like a first domino. *If this happened, I think so many good things would follow.* Once you make headway on one win, you can repeat the pattern on a new win.

So what's your finish line? What's your win?

With crystal clear clarity, what specifically do you want to do and by when?

Write down your goal and tell someone. If you don't write it down, you have a wish, not a goal. So write it down *and* tell someone.

Dr. Gail Matthews, a psychology professor at Dominican University, reports that people who write down goals are significantly more likely to achieve them. If you write down your goal and tell a friend, your likelihood increases even more.[12]

Goals give direction. Without direction, we are running a race with no finish line.

Goals Give Inspiration

We've all seen the "before and after" pictures that tout a particular diet. If you're debating whether to start a new plan, that "after" picture will inspire you. *Yes! That's what I want to look like! That's my goal. I'm going for it!* Goals motivate.

The apostle Paul had lots of inspiration. When Christianity started, he was a young Pharisee who hated the upstart Jesus movement and everything it represented. Paul participated in the murder of Christians and traveled from town to town persecuting them.

On a trip to Damascus in pursuit of more converts, lightning suddenly flashed around him. He fell to the ground, and Jesus spoke to him, out loud, from heaven. Jesus asked, "Saul, Saul, why do you persecute me?" (Acts 9:4). Jesus and Paul had a brief but life-changing conversation. Then Paul got up, and he was blind!

That's crazy! You know the words to "Amazing Grace"?

> Amazing grace (how sweet the sound)
> that saved a wretch like me!
> I once was lost, but now am found
> was blind, but now I see.[13]

For Paul it was, "I once was lost, but now I'm found; I could see, but now I'm blind!" He eventually got his vision back, but, wow, what a moment.

Paul's life was eternally changed by God's unconditional love. God treated him with grace even though Paul had been trying to stop people from becoming Christians. No wonder Paul ended up with a life goal of sharing God's grace in the hope that people would become Christ's followers. Here's his explanation of what led to the win he set for his life: "You know what I was like when I followed the Jewish religion—how I violently persecuted God's church. I did my best to destroy it. I was far ahead of my fellow Jews in my zeal for the traditions of my ancestors. But even before I was born, God chose me and called me by his marvelous grace. Then it pleased him to reveal his Son to me so that I would proclaim the Good News about Jesus to the Gentiles" (Galatians 1:13–16 NLT).

Paul had a specific goal, and that goal gave him inspiration.

When I defined the win of prioritizing time with my kids, that motivated me to seek out those opportunities. I would walk through the house, on the lookout for a bored child who was ready to hang out.

Goals are important, and your journey to reach them begins when you define that win. But let's be clear: defining the win is not *how* you win.

How do you win?

The answer may surprise you. It's counterintuitive, but this truth can set you free. There's more power in it than I can possibly describe.

Are you ready? Here it is.

You win when you quit trying.

Exercise 8

Complete the following sentence.

The primary aspects of my life where I need to establish a win are:

> Examples: my marriage, career, relationship with God,
> health, finances, parenting.

Using the areas of your life in which you want to establish a win, work through this next part of the exercise to define it. Refer back to my examples at the beginning of the chapter if needed.

You can repeat this pattern for each win you want to establish. If you need more or fewer than three steps, feel free to list whatever it takes.

My new win is to:

Using what you have written here, state your goal and who you will tell for support.

My goal is:

and I commit to share this with:

Principle 8

**Defining your win is how you begin. Write
down your goal and tell someone.**

Run to win!

—1 Corinthians 9:24 NLT

2.2 Trying versus Training

People can have the same goals yet get vastly different results.

No married couple starts out saying, "We're just hoping to endure the next fifty years. We may hate each other the whole time, but it's fine as long as we don't get divorced." No. Every marriage begins with the same goal: "We want to be happily married forever!" But half of all marriages end in divorce.

No guy ends his high school sports career thinking, "In twenty years I would love to have high cholesterol and maybe even prediabetes!" No. Every guy assumes he's going to be able to see at least one ab in his forties. But about half of middle-aged men in the US are overweight or obese.

No one says, "Someday I want to be buried under debt I can't repay, debating whether I should declare bankruptcy." No. Everyone wants to enjoy financial freedom and be able to give generously to important causes. But the reality is that more than 60 percent of the US population is living paycheck to paycheck, and the average household debt is more than $130,000.[14]

No sports team begins the season with the goal, "This year we're hoping to come in third place!" No. Every team wants to win the championship. But only one will hold up the trophy at the end of the season.

Same starting goals, yet drastically varying results.

I know I just encouraged you by saying, "Choose your finish line!

Define your win!" And you should. But we also need to acknowledge the limitations of goals.

To recap—defining the win *is* how you begin. But defining the win is not how you win.

How do you win?

You quit trying.

What do winners do differently? What does the couple who celebrates thirty years of marriage do? What does the healthy, fit forty-year-old do? How about the family with no debt and with savings in the bank? The sports team standing on the podium?

They don't try.

They train.

> **Winners don't try.
> They train.**

Paul had a goal, but he also had direction and inspiration. Having a goal was not enough. Paul focused on training. Let's continue where we left off with his talk about athletes in the Olympic and Isthmian Games: "Everyone who competes in the games goes into strict training" (1 Cor. 9:25).

The competitor's "strict training" was intense. The Greek philosopher Epictetus, who lived at the same time as Paul, wrote that the athlete's training "involves thirst and broiling heat and swallowing handfuls of sand."[15] *Seriously?* When I played sports in high school and college, we sometimes had to run wind sprints, but we never had to swallow sand! If Coach told us, "Today, we're eating sand!" I would have said, "Coach, I'm switching to band. Playing the oboe suddenly seems cool."

Obviously, what those athletes endured was no joke. It probably made some of them want to quit. But Epictetus tells us that if an athlete withdrew "without sufficient reason," they would be "whipped."[16] (I don't even want to think about my high school coach whipping me because of my oboe decision.)

Paul used that level of training to describe the type of training he embraced to move toward his finish line. "I discipline my body like an athlete, training it to do what it should. Otherwise, I fear that after preaching to others I myself might be disqualified" (1 Cor. 9:27 NLT).

The word translated "discipline" is the Greek word *hypopiazo*, literally meaning "to hit under the eye." Paul chose an intense word to declare that he would do whatever it took to win.

Paul continued, "Training [his body] to do what it should." The word "training" is from the Greek *doulagogo*, which means "to enslave." Paul would not let his body, his thoughts, his emotions, his passions, or his feelings determine his actions. He was running his race and would do whatever it took to meet his goal.

Paul entered into a life of training and encouraged others to do the same. He told his ministry apprentice Timothy, "Train yourself to be godly" (1 Tim. 4:7). The word translated "train" is the Greek word *gymnazo*. The literal meaning is "to exercise naked." *What?! We just went from a G to a PG-13 rating!* Yes, the Greek athletes preparing to compete in the games trained naked. Why? Because they didn't want anything to get in their way or slow them down. If you've ever watched the Olympics and questioned some of the attire—or lack thereof—now you have a better understanding of the reasoning *and* history.

Just to offer a disclaimer here: I am not encouraging you to show up at the gym in your birthday suit. But as Christ followers working toward change, we do need to embrace a life of training while getting rid of anything that slows our growth.

We want to achieve our goal.

We will not let anything get in our way or slow us down.

Paul defined his win. He had a goal, which gave him direction and inspiration. But a goal is not enough because winners and losers often begin with the same goals.

You've had goals. You've been desperate to change. So you've tried. You've really tried.

That's the problem. Trying doesn't work. You've been trying for too long. Trying never achieves consistent results. We've seen it time and time again. The vicious cycle:

- You try.
- You get tired of trying.
- You quit.
- You feel embarrassed.
- You regroup.
- You try.
- You get tired of trying.
- (You know the drill.)

Trying doesn't work. Training does.

In the classic Star Wars film *The Empire Strikes Back*, Master Yoda tells the young Jedi Luke during training, "You must unlearn what you have learned." Luke replies, "All right, I'll give it a try." Yoda, frustrated, demands, "No! Try not. Do or do not. There is no try."[17]

We are going to change. We are going to achieve our goals through training, not trying.

What's the difference?

To *try* is to attempt to do the right thing by exerting effort in the moment.

To *train* is to commit to developing strategic habits that equip you to do the right thing in the moment.

To finally experience the change and victory we desire, it's essential that we understand the difference between trying and training. So read those definitions again until you've got it.

Let's say you have a trying-based approach to change. The "moment" arrives. Like it usually does every day. You will have the opportunity to do the good thing you want to do. Or you will be hit with the temptation to do the bad thing you don't want to do. In that moment, you will remember your goal. So you'll muster all your willpower and determination and hope it's enough to change.

If you commit to a training-based approach to change, it's not about the moment but about what you do before the moment comes. You engage in strategic habits, in deliberate disciplines, that equip you to be ready when the opportunity or temptation arises. If you train, when the moment arrives, you won't need to try nearly as hard as you used to, and you'll get better results!

Remember my example of when I was successfully eating healthy all day and then blowing it at night? I was trying. Really hard. But I wasn't getting anywhere. When I finally developed a plan for the nighttime—engaging in training at night like I did during the day—I got results. I ate a full and healthy dinner early in the evening. Then I found some healthy, low-calorie snacks to replace the junk food. Sometimes, I would go on a walk to distract myself. I stopped trying and started training.

As I have lived this, I've wondered if another, more subtle, distinction is that trying can prevent relying. When I try, I do what I can in *my* strength. Trying can keep me from allowing God to give me *his* strength so he can do in and through me what I cannot.

By trying, I may be unintentionally denying God's gracious offer to make his power perfect in my weakness (2 Cor. 12:9). Trying can, in a sense, be a denying of God. Training done right is a partnership with God.

> **Stop trying and start training.**

Do you want to change? To achieve your win? Stop trying and start training.

Here's one more definition of training that should be helpful: training is doing today what you can do today so that you can do tomorrow what you can't do today.

I do today what I can do today through "strategic habits." So that I can do tomorrow what I can't do today—avoid temptation and advance toward my goal.

Winning comes through training, not trying.

While this principle is obvious in so many areas of life, people often miss what's most important. When it comes to "finish line" areas, Christians tend to have a theology of trying. We think we can get where we want to go by simply giving more effort. We're convinced this works:

- "I'm going to try to be closer to God."
- "We're going to try to have a good marriage."
- "I'm going to try to be a better parent."
- "We're going to try to stop having sex before marriage."
- "I'm going to try to be a more loving person."

Yet when that's our approach, we set ourselves up for failure.

Trying doesn't work. Training does.

We know this: You don't get an A in school by showing up for the final exam and trying hard. You get the good grade by committing to strategic habits (going to class, taking notes, studying) before the test. Those equip you to do the right thing (have the right answers) in the moment when you take the test. Day by day, you do what you can do today (go to class, study) so you can do tomorrow what you can't do today (get an A on the test).

Another example: Paul referred to running a race in the games. Imagine you have a goal to run a marathon. But let's say right now, where you are is thirty-five pounds overweight. You have not run since eighth grade. You haven't exercised in years. Last night for dinner you had Twinkies. For dessert you had, well, more Twinkies.

But you really want to run a marathon, so you sign up. The

day of the race you're stoked. You take your place in the crowd of runners. Before the gun goes off, the person standing next to you introduces herself. She asks how long you've been training.

You respond, "Training? Well, I haven't. I haven't actually run since eighth grade!"

"Really? That's interesting." She sounds dubious. Then asks, "Hey, what's that on your shirt?"

You look down, "Oh, that's . . . Twinkie filling. I guess some squirted out during my prerace breakfast."

She seems confused. "Are you feeling confident you'll be able to finish this marathon?"

"Yeah!" you smile and announce, "Because I'm going to try really hard!"

She questions you. "You're going to *try* really hard?"

You fearlessly respond, "Yup!" then snap a quick selfie to capture the moment, you know, just in case you set a course record.

The starting gun fires. The runners take off. You didn't train, but now in the race, you try really hard. Are you going to make it? No. Before long, you'll be lying on the side of the road, throwing up and crying for your mommy.

Why? Because you tried really hard, but you did not train. The only way you'll go from being out of shape to being able to run a marathon is by training. By committing to strategic habits before the marathon that equip you to run the marathon. By doing today what you can do today (maybe running a mile) so that you can do tomorrow what you can't do today (maybe running a mile and a half). Keep practicing your strategic habits, and you will reach your goal of running a marathon. Trying tends to be a momentary reaction, while training is an ongoing action.

We need to apply this principle to our most important priorities. Training, not trying, is how you:

- Get closer to God
- Have an awesome marriage
- Raise great kids
- Forgive the person who hurt you
- Develop closer friendships
- Become more patient
- Win your fantasy football league
- Get better sleep
- Spend less time on your phone
- Improve your leadership skills
- Read through the Bible in a year
- Develop your guitar playing
- Stop looking at porn
- Learn how to crack an egg with one hand
- (Insert your number one goal)

So a little review. How are you going to finally achieve your win? You'll do this by remembering:

1. Who. Not do.
2. You do what you do because of what you think of you.
3. To change what you do, you need to first change what you think of you.
4. You are who God says you are.
5. You *will* change, and you *can* become who you want to become.
6. If your do is about who God wants you to become—about who you want to become—then your do is not small.
7. Defining your win is how you begin. You need a goal. Write down your goal and tell someone.
8. And achieving your goal is about training. Not trying.

Chances are if you have struggled to change, you've been trying for too long, and trying never achieves consistent results. Too often, trying leads to quitting. So quit trying.

In the last exercise, I asked you to define your win and share it with someone. Now you know you have to achieve that win through training. So what training (habits, relationships, actions) do you need to do to achieve what you want most?

That leads us to the next crucial question: What one strategic habit will have the most impact in leading you to your win?

Exercise 9

Using the defined wins from exercise 8, write down some ways you have tried to change in the past but failed. This is important to identify what you've done that has not worked—the trying.

Taking those same defined wins, list some strategic habits you could implement through training.

Examples:

To forgive someone who hurt you, you can train by (1) writing out the verses where Jesus taught on forgiveness and (2) writing out the offenses that God and others have forgiven you for.

To read your Bible every day, you can train by (1) waking up twenty minutes earlier and (2) setting your Bible out each night in a visible place as a reminder, open to the last passage you read.

Last, how could giving up trying and focusing on training be freeing for you?

Principle 9

Trying doesn't work. Training does.

**Trying is an attempt to do the right thing
by exerting effort in the moment.**

**Training is a commitment to strategic habits
you do before the moment that equip you
to do the right thing in the moment.**

All athletes are disciplined in their training.
They do it to win a prize that will fade away, but we
do it for an eternal prize. So I run with purpose in
every step. . . . I discipline my body like an athlete,
training it to do what it should.

—1 Corinthians 9:25–27 NLT

2.3 Discipline Is Not a Dirty Word

I have a bit of training in the martial arts. I am very familiar with Daniel LaRusso aka the Karate Kid and the Cobra Kai dojo. I can wax on, wax off with the best of them. Given an opportunity, I can sweep your leg so fast your head will spin. For about fifteen years, I dreamed of taking up jujitsu. I was enamored with how beautiful and amazing the sport is and how the fighters have swagger like Jagger.

My friend Bobby got tired of hearing me moan about how I'm too old to take up jujitsu. One day, he surprised me with, "Craig, I'm going to take jujitsu classes. You want to go?" *For real? Yes!*

We took two classes together and then Bobby quit. That's when I realized he had set me up.

Jujitsu has been exhilarating and . . . interesting. When I started, someone at the gym told me I needed a "gi," pronounced like *geese* with no *s*. I thought that was some kind of butter, as in ghee. But no. A gi is basically an oversized, heavy cotton bathrobe. I felt oddly cool in my gi until I found out I could not tie the drawstring.[18] I don't have an engineering degree and could not master the pull-it-backward-before-you-pull-it-forward maneuver (*#thestruggleisreal*). During my first lesson, my pants kept falling down. I had expected to be embarrassed because I sucked at jujitsu, not because I sucked at jujitsu with my pants around my ankles.

There was a lot to remember. I constantly forgot to bring my belt to my lessons. Jujitsu people frown on beltless fighters. A jujitsu fighter without a belt is kind of like Ben and Jerry without the ice cream.

Even if I did remember my belt, I usually forgot to bow when I stepped onto the mat. Jujitsu has official traditions, including bowing to your opponent as you bump fists and then swipe hands. I had zero experience bowing with a set of simultaneous hand gestures. (If my family tells you they caught me practicing bowing and fist-bumping in the mirror, they're lying.)

Besides all the stated rules, jujitsu also has an unwritten code. An "open mat" is an unstructured training session where you can "roll" against anyone. Rolling is like sparring; students practice fighting each other. The unwritten rule is that students with lower belts do not ask more advanced higher belts to roll. Some people in the jujitsu world consider that a sign of disrespect. If a lower belt asks a higher belt to roll, the higher belt will go extra hard to teach the lower belt a lesson.

No one told me that little detail.

I was excited to practice my new skills. I'm a friendly guy. I approached some dude sporting a well-worn brown belt. "Hiiii! How's it going? I'm Craig! Wanna roll?" I noticed his demeanor didn't match my energy. I was pleasant and warm. He seemed, well, agitated and hostile. *Ruh-roh.*

About a minute later, he smashed my head so deep into the mat that I wondered if I'd fused into it. I left the ring with my ear swollen to half the size of Texas. (But no matter what you've heard, I did *not* scream like a little kid. That was someone else.)

I was discouraged, but I refused to be defeated. (Well, he did defeat me, but I was not defeated in spirit.) I continued to learn and practice the disciplines of jujitsu—the written *and* unwritten code.

My training in jujitsu often feels counterintuitive.

I thought I'd have advantages because I'm on the stronger side and have some natural athletic ability. I've played a lot of sports. I tried to rely on those abilities until I realized they were working against me. What I thought were assets turned out to be liabilities. Jujitsu is about flow and technique, not just strength and speed.

My instinct was to go into full-on Incredible Hulk mode against an opponent, as in, "You wouldn't like me when I'm angry!"

That is not the way of jujitsu. At all. You fight relaxed and learn to breathe slowly.

Trying hard did not work, so I entered into a life of training. I take three private lessons a week, watch videos, and train at home. Early on, I quickly realized I had to stop trying and start learning the disciplines of jujitsu.

I also had to master my grips. Grips are the tactics you use to control and move your opponent, such as ball-and-socket, gable, and pretzel, to name a few. Each grip has its own insanely intricate steps, and I was completely inept at first. (Even with my drawstring—uh, belt—tied.) But I continued to train. I did today what I could do today. And then one tomorrow, it all came together. Finally, I could do what I couldn't do. That felt so good. *Freedom!*

Training by doing daily disciplines led me from incompetence to mastery. (Okay, I'm not a master yet, but it seems that way compared to that first pants-less day when my bleeding face was stuffed six inches into a mat.)

Jujitsu is all about discipline.

For Christ followers, making changes—putting sin behind us, growing in maturity, accomplishing a goal, achieving success—is all about discipline.

You probably have your own jujitsu—some hobby, sport, activity, or skill that allows you to relate to my experience. That same journey from rookie to expert has to happen with any aspect of life where we want real change.

You may be gagging right now because you hate the idea of discipline. You might feel about discipline the same way you would about using sandpaper for toilet paper. I mention discipline and you wonder whether you should use this book to start a fire in your Big Green Egg smoker.

Believe me, I get it. But hold up.

Discipline has a bad rap. The word *discipline* makes us think of doing things we don't want to do, like getting up early, making the bed, and eating brussels sprouts.

You may also believe you are not disciplined and could never be disciplined.

I want to give you a definition of discipline that changed my life. One that helps you see discipline as attainable and attractive because it's the path to achieving your goals. Ready?

> **Discipline is choosing what you want most over what you want now.**

Discipline is choosing what you want most over what you want now.

There's always something we want now. That *now* desire is seductive because it promises instant gratification. But those promises rarely deliver.

There is also something we want most. That *most* desire rarely provides instant gratification. But it offers you something far more important—the life you want to live. Discipline is choosing what you want most over what you want now. Let's walk through some examples.

Marriage

What you want most: a happy marriage filled with love and intimacy.

What you want now: to watch TV.

You know watching TV will not help you have a happy marriage. Having couch-conversation time with your spouse will help you have a happy marriage. Discipline is choosing what you want most ("Let's take twenty minutes to talk before we turn on the TV.") over what you want now ("What are we gonna watch tonight?"). It's easier to choose what you want now, but you live the life you want by choosing what you want most.

Finances

What you want most: to be out of debt so money is not a stress, to experience financial peace, and to give generously.

What you want now: to buy the new refrigerator you saw at your friend's house. After all, it connects to the internet, and the light inside comes on when you tap on the door!

You know spending $1,800 on a new refrigerator will not lead to financial freedom. Sticking with your boring, no-wifi refrigerator will help you dig out of your money pit. Discipline is choosing what you want most ("We've committed to spend less money. Our refrigerator is fine.") over what you want now ("Let's get the new fridge! It might allow us to email our meats and cheeses!"). It's easier to choose what you want now, but you live the life you want by choosing what you want most.

Spiritually

What you want most: a great relationship with God that leads you to have a life of meaning, joy, and peace.

What you want now: to sleep for ten more minutes.

You know hitting snooze does not translate into intimacy with God. Getting out of bed to spend some time reading the Bible or praying will grow your relationship with God. Discipline is choosing what you want most ("I am going to go splash cold water on my face, get coffee into my bloodstream, and read my Bible.") over what you want now ("I love God, but I also love my pillow. Where is that snooze button?"). It's easier to choose what you want now, but you live the life you want by choosing what you want most.

Purity

What you want most: to be pure so you can have an unhindered relationship with God and with your spouse (or future spouse).

What you want now: to look at those images on your phone or have sex ASAP.

You know going to that website or those accounts on Instagram will not help you be pure and will lead to shame. Calling your accountability partner instead of looking at porn will help you be more intimate with God and your spouse (or future spouse).

Discipline is choosing what you want most ("I'm tempted again. Can you pray for me? Call me tomorrow and ask if I looked!") over what you want now ("I can't help it. I'm human. I've got needs."). It's easier to choose what you want now, but you live the life you want by choosing what you want most.

■ ■ ■

Training instead of trying means choosing discipline.

Discipline means choosing what you want most over what you want now.

To experience real and lasting change, to finally live the life you want, you choose discipline.

The problem is you don't want to. Well, at least in the moment you don't. Right now, discipline feels painful.

- Going to the gym when you want to play video games feels painful.
- Choosing not to check out the person with the great body at the gym feels painful.
- Putting down your phone so you can focus on the person in the room with you feels painful.

No one likes pain. Why would you choose pain?

Because, either way, there's pain. You *have* to choose pain. But you *get* to choose *what kind* of pain.

The writer of Hebrews speaks of this exact concept in chapter 12, verse 11, "No discipline is enjoyable while it is happening—it's painful! But afterward there will be a peaceful harvest of right living for those who are trained in this way" (NLT). Note the words—"discipline," "painful," "right living," and "trained."

You are going to experience pain. Discipline may feel painful, but if you don't live a disciplined life, you will experience the pain of regret. Not choosing what you want now feels painful. But if you do choose what you want now, you will later experience the pain of not having what you want most.

For example, when you were a kid, obeying your parents often felt painful. But if you didn't, you experienced the pain of consequences later.

In school, studying was a total pain. But not studying led to the pain of failing a test or even having to retake a class.

Saying no to temptation feels painful. But if you say yes, you go through the pain of guilt. You may also end up having to free yourself from the claws of an addiction. And then there's one of the worst emotions a human can feel—shame.

As a parent, when you're worn out from your job and stressed out by life, taking the time to spiritually invest in your kids can feel painful. But if you don't, you may experience the pain of having grown-up kids who resent you or have drifted away from God. While that can happen to the best of parents, because all kids have free will, investing in your kids when they are young increases your chances of what Proverbs 22:6 states: "Direct your children onto the right path, and when they are older, they will not leave it" (NLT). That directing can be painful!

The bottom line is you can't avoid pain.

The question is: Will you choose the pain of discipline or the pain of regret?

I have found the pain of regret is always worse than the pain of discipline. Pain along the way is far preferable to getting down the road and realizing you missed out on some important aspect of the life God had for you.

Let's choose the pain of discipline and refuse the pain of regret. Let's commit to never having to say:

- "I should have taken better care of myself."
- "I wish I had never started down that path. I had no idea how it would ruin my life."
- "If only I had forgiven my parent. Now it's too late."
- "I never planned on ending up here. I'd give anything for another chance."

Desire alone won't get you what you want most, but discipline will. So don't avoid the pain of discipline. If you do, not getting what you want most will be your biggest regret.

You may think, *If discipline is what I need, I'm in trouble, because I'm not disciplined.*

Not true. You actually are disciplined.

If you look at the areas of your life where you are struggling, I suspect you'll see a lack of discipline. In Proverbs 25:28, we read, "A person without self-control is like a city with broken-down walls" (NLT).

> **Desire alone won't get you what you want most, but discipline will.**

But if you look at the areas of your life where you are winning, I bet you'll see you are disciplined. Training works, and there are pockets of your life where you are seeing that work. What's true in your life is true in everyone's life: the path to public success is always paved with private discipline.

I like the way Joe Frazier, a heavyweight champion boxer in the 1960s and '70s, puts it: "You can map out a fight plan or a life plan, but when the action starts, you're down to your reflexes. That's where your roadwork shows. If you cheated on that in the dark of the morning, you're getting found out now under the bright lights."[19]

People saw Smokin' Joe in the ring winning championship fights. They didn't see Frazier running miles every day before the sun came up. The path to public success is always paved with private discipline.

Here's a simple example: You have to be in a wedding. Hours before, you shower or bathe and work on your hair. You spend extra time to look your absolute best. When you walk in and people compliment you, they are actually recognizing what you did in private to look the way you do in public.

Think of discipline as choosing to do what's important to you. You repeatedly do some things that are important to you. You eat. You sleep. Those are disciplines.

You probably have some disciplines that are not helping you win. You may stress eat, oversleep, play hours of video games every night, or check your phone 160 times a day.

Those are also disciplines. You've trained yourself to do those things.

Proof that you can be disciplined. You are disciplined.

Now it's time to be disciplined—to choose what you want most over what you want now—in the most important parts of your life where you want change.

Why?

Because your desires don't determine who you become.

Your disciplines do.

Exercise 10

Identify the top three areas in your life where you feel you lack discipline.

1.

2.

3.

Next, identify the top three areas in your life where you exhibit the most discipline.

1.

2.

3.

In the parts of your life where you are choosing what you want now over what you want most, write down your reasons for why you may be putting off the pain of discipline and risking the pain of regret.

Examples: I'm just too tired to be consistent in disciplining my kids. I'm healthy right now, so I have time to start working out down the road.

In the areas where you realize you lack discipline, what is the biggest positive change that could come if you chose some pain today over putting it off until tomorrow?

Principle 10

Discipline is choosing what you want most over what you want now.

The path to public success is always paved with private discipline.

No discipline is enjoyable while it is happening—it's painful! But afterward there will be a peaceful harvest of right living for those who are trained in this way.

—Hebrews 12:11 NLT

2.4 Your Habit and a Plot Twist

Previously, I asked you, What do you most need to do to have what you want most?

Now I want to flip the question to this: What do you most need to stop doing to have what you want most?

We are going to learn how to start *and* stop habits. To begin, let's identify the habits we need to start and stop to achieve our goals. You may want to choose one strategic habit to start and one not-so-strategic habit to stop.

> **Identify the habits you need to start and stop to achieve your goals.**

Here are some examples to help you wrap your brain around how this might work:

- Goal: get closer to God.
  - Habit to start: reading the Bible every day or attending a small-group Bible study.
  - Habit to stop: hitting snooze in the morning or planning things on the weekend that prevent church attendance.
- Goal: get out of debt.
  - Habit to start: following a biblically based money management course, such as Financial Peace University.
  - Habit to stop: purchasing without praying or making only minimum credit card payments.

- Goal: make more friends.
  - ► Habit to start: participating in a group, a team, or a hobby that can be done only with others.
  - ► Habit to stop: binge-watching TV alone every weekend.
- Goal: improve your marriage.
  - ► Habit to start: doing a couples devotional together every evening or committing to a weekly date night.
  - ► Habit to stop: blaming your spouse or talking negatively about your spouse to other people.
- Goal: get a promotion at work.
  - ► Habit to start: setting clear goals and documenting achievements to share in an upcoming review.
  - ► Habit to stop: talking negatively about coworkers or engaging in office politics or gossip.

See how this works?

We think we need to change our results. So we make goals like "Lose twenty pounds" or "Improve my marriage" or "Get promoted at work." And we really want those things, so we try. Then we get frustrated because the results are not happening the way we want or as fast as we want. So finally, we just quit.

Why do we fail? Because we try.

Instead, we should train by ascertaining the strategic habits we need to start and stop. What can we do to move, little by little, toward our wins? We then need the discipline to do these things, to choose what we want most over what we want now.

So what is your win?

What strategic habit will lead to your win?

That's what you need to decide.

Now are you ready for a plot twist?

This may not rank up with the best movie plot twists like these:

- Bruce Willis was dead the whole time.
- Darth Vader is Luke's father.
- Norman Bates is his mother.
- That limping guy is Keyser Söze.
- The murderer in *Scream* is actually two people.
- The two dudes in *Fight Club* are actually one person.

But this plot twist is legit.

Seriously, are you ready for the "I didn't see that coming" plot twist?

Assuming you are, here we go: you win when you make *doing* your habit your win.

Wait. What? I thought I had a win, then a habit to lead me toward my win.

Yes, that is true. But if you focus on your win, more often than not, you will feel like you are losing. If you focus on your habit, you can win every day.

With a training-not-trying approach, you make doing your habit your win. This one choice will turn your attempts to change upside down.

Let's say your win is to eliminate $20,000 in credit-card debt. You plan to do this using a debt-snowball strategy. So you create these habits:

1. Developing and adhering to a realistic monthly budget
2. Paying an extra $100 a month on your credit-card debt
3. Not eating out or buying expensive coffee until the debt is paid off
4. Using only your debit card or cash to make purchases

How long will it take to pay off $20,000 in credit-card debt?

Thirty years to never if you just keep making the minimum payments. You could pay an additional $30,000 to $60,000 depending on interest rates. But if you follow your debt-snowball strategy, you should be able to pay off the debt in a few years and also save tens of thousands in interest.

You might be disheartened every time you get your credit-card statement and wonder, *Why is it taking so long to pay this off?* You may feel like it's never going to happen and be tempted to quit.

Accomplishing your goal could take a few years. But you *can* do your habits every day. You can choose not to eat out. You can choose to make your coffee at home instead of buying it on the way to work. You can take all that money you are saving and apply it to your credit-card debt. If you do those habits every day, they will eventually lead to your goal.

Many recovery programs use the phrase, "Make the next right choice." The focus has to be taken off how long it will take and placed on what can be done now.

As the wisest man on the planet, King Solomon always nailed one-liners. Ecclesiastes 7:8 is no exception: "The end of a matter is better than its beginning, and patience is better than pride."

So if you make doing the habit your win, you can win every day.

Perhaps your win is to lose twenty pounds. Your habits are eating a hundred fewer calories than you burn each day and going for a walk at lunchtime.

How long will it take to lose twenty pounds? Many experts say slow and steady is the best approach for lasting weight loss. The Centers for Disease Control and Prevention tell us losing a pound a week is healthy.[20]

Losing the weight might take five months. That means you would have about 150 days of not yet achieving your goal. Losing a pound a week might feel like *not* losing weight for 150 days.

But you can do your habits every day. Whether they help you pay off credit-card debt, lose weight, or accomplish any start or stop, if you consistently do your habits, they will eventually lead to your goal. If you make doing the habit your win, you can win every day.

In business terms, we might refer to this as inputs and outcomes. The inputs (processes) are what you do every day. Those inputs become a pathway that lead you toward a new place. The outcome is the result of the inputs.

> If you make doing the habit your win, you can win every day.

Obsessing over outcomes is easy. A car dealership that typically sells eighty cars a month might set a goal of selling a hundred. That's an outcome. The problem is the dealership can't really control the outcome. The car salespeople might try harder but will probably get the same results and grow tired of trying. They can't control outcomes, but they can control inputs. That dealership can have every salesperson call ten former customers. Or offer each person who buys a car a gift if they put a review online. Or try various customer incentives, monitoring which have the greatest impact. Those are inputs, which can be controlled. The right inputs will lead to the right outcomes.

Inputs and outcomes may be business terms, but businesses aren't alone in obsessing over outcomes. We make New Year's resolutions like, "Get a promotion" or "Quit drinking" or "Spend more time with my kids." Those are outcomes. We don't want to focus on outcomes. They can take a while to achieve, and we may feel like we're losing along the way. We also can't control all the outcomes. You can't control whether your boss will give you a promotion or your kids will want to spend time with you.

Sometimes we obsess over outcomes in other people's lives. We envy their outcomes. "I wish we had a marriage like they have." "It would be amazing to be financially free like my neighbor." "She seems so close to God. Why can't I be more like her?" We can so easily see other people's outcomes. But what we can't see is what they do every day. Private discipline paves the way to public success. Instead of envying outcomes, we'd be wise to imitate inputs.

Make doing your habit your win. Obsess over the process instead of the outcome. You don't get results by focusing on results. You get results by focusing on the actions that get results.

This is freeing! Do you feel it? You should be yelling, "Freeeedom!" like William Wallace at the end of *Braveheart*. (Well, when William Wallace was yelling, "Freedom!" he was being executed, so let's not get carried away with the comparison.) This is freeing because you can't control every outcome. You can't control how many cars you'll sell this month or how much weight you'll lose. But you can control your actions right now.

Your goal might be to become a great public speaker. But it may take you some time to get to that win. What you can do is watch one TED Talk a day, taking notes on what you should apply. You can write a new ten-minute talk every week. You can film yourself giving your ten-minute talk, then watch it, looking for what you can improve.

With a training-not-trying approach, you choose strategic habits, and you consider every day you engage in your process a win.

That is something you can do. That is freedom. And those right inputs will eventually lead to your desired outcome.

You. Will. Win!

Let me relieve your fear, because I bet it's on your mind: you don't have to win every day to win overall.

So you discover you need to choose a strategic habit. You learn the key to achieving your goal is doing the habit every day. Then you hear a voice whisper, *Every day? You can't do that. You know you won't be able to do it every day.*

In the next section, we will learn how to make our habits so easy and attractive we will want to do them every day. But, even still, it is probably true that you won't be able to do them every day. So thank God you don't have to win every day to win. That's exactly why the apostle Paul talked about grace so much in his letters. You are not going to be perfect. No one is perfect. I like what James Clear says: "Habits are behaviors that we repeat consistently. However, they are not behaviors that we repeat perfectly. This small idea—that consistency does not require perfection—is important."[21]

The world won't end if you miss a day. Don't judge yourself. If you miss today, just start back with your habit tomorrow. You'll get there eventually if more days are wins than not, right? If you do your habit, not perfectly but consistently, you will get to your goal.

Stop focusing on the goal. Make doing the habit your win. Obsess over the process, always reminding yourself:

I'm in training.

It will take some time to get where I want to go, but every day I am getting closer.

Every day I do my habit, I win.

That's success.

Exercise 11

I want you to do the exercise I introduced at the beginning of this chapter. Repeat the template as many times as you need.

Here's a reminder of one of the examples:

Goal: get closer to God.

Habit to start: reading the Bible every day or attending a small-group Bible study.

Habit to stop: hitting snooze in the morning or planning things on the weekend that prevent church attendance.

Goal:

Habit to start:

Habit to stop:

Complete the following sentence.

When I have a day where I don't win, to stay on track, I commit to:

Example: Not miss more than one day; tell my
accountability partner.

Principle 11

Make doing your habit your win.

You don't have to win every day to win.

The end of a matter is better than its beginning,
and patience is better than pride.

—Ecclesiastes 7:8

2.5 I'm in Training

I told you about one of my first jujitsu rolls when I unknowingly challenged a higher belt who punished my face for disrespecting him.

Well, here's the rest of the story:

After that first fight, I started winning. And winning. And winning. I rolled against a champion wrestler and won. I fought against black belts and won. I challenged my coach (who holds a gold medal from a worldwide jujitsu competition) and won.

Well, not exactly.

If you watched, you would say I got my butt kicked every time. I was whipped by a 220-pound NCAA collegiate wrestler. (I might have been whipped by a fourteen-year-old boy who was at least fifty pounds lighter than I am, but there are no witnesses to prove it.) I was pinned, choked, smashed, and twisted into unusually awkward positions with other guys. Turns out those positions are horribly painful and impossible to escape.

From your perspective, if you saw some massive guy sitting on my head or me repeatedly tapping out, you'd say I was losing. And losing. And losing. But I would say I was winning. And winning. And winning. Why?

I started jujitsu at the age of fifty-two. I now have three stripes on my white belt and am closing in on four. Because I keep showing up. My confidence keeps increasing. And as my confidence grows, by the nature of the sport's code, my humility grows too.[22]

My mind is sharper. I keep improving my skills, including all of those crazy grips. (These days my pants almost never fall down midfight.)

No matter how the results on the mats appear, I am not losing. I am winning. Because I'm in training.

This is a great place to stop and remind yourself, *I'm in training. It will take some time to get where I want to go, but every day I am getting closer. And every day I do my habit, I win. That's success to me.*

> **I'm in training.**

"I'm in training" is an important phrase for change.

You consistently engage in your strategic habit. You haven't yet achieved your goal. But you continue to run with purpose, knowing, "I'm in training."

This connects back to the *who before do* idea that identity drives behavior.

When I'm trying, it's like I keep hoping to become something I'm not. But when I'm training, I keep getting better at what I already am!

I'm not trying. I'm in training!

- "We aren't trying to have a better marriage. Ours is a great marriage in training."
- "Oh, no thanks, I can't have a donut. I'm in training."
- "I slipped up and looked at Instagram, comparing what others have with what I have. But I know that's not who I am. I am a content, non-comparer in training!"
- "No, we can't sleep in and skip church. We're in spiritual training."
- "I'm all alone; I could look at porn. But I won't 'cause I'm in training."
- "I may never be as spiritually mature as my small-group leader, but I am in training to become who God made me to be."

So what are we going to do?

1. *Focus on who before do.* We know behavior modification doesn't work, so we're all about identity transformation.
2. *Define our wins.* We need the direction of a goal to help us begin.
3. *Train, not try.* We will embrace a strategic habit and quit a habit we need to stop. Every day we'll live disciplined lives by choosing what we want most over what we want now.

Can you feel the power of embracing this new way to think about and believe in change?

You're focusing on inputs, not outcomes. It's a plot shift. A game changer that works!

If the idea of starting and sticking to a habit, or of being able to stop doing what you keep doing, sounds intimidating or undoable, take heart; we're going to attack that in part 3.

But now you understand that you don't have to wait six weeks or six months or six years to win. You aren't successful just when you achieve your goal in the future. You are successful when you train today. When you're training, you're winning. And you can win every day!

> I'm successful when I train today.

You may not get to your goal as soon as you want. The pace of change might be a little slower than you like. You might trip up a few times as you walk toward victory. But engaging this plan will work. You will have the power to change and will see real change happen.

You'll have peace with the process because:

You're in training!

Exercise 12

Using the goals and the habits to start and stop from exercise 11, complete these sentences:

I am going to stop trying to [blank] by:

I am starting my training by:

For each sentence, create a statement to remind you about your training.

> Example: I am not trying to get healthy. I am exercising regularly, saying no to sweets, and going to bed early because I am in training.

Principle 12

I am not trying.

I am in training!

Physical training is good, but training for godliness is much better, promising benefits in this life and in the life to come.

—1 Timothy 4:8 NLT

Part 3

Habits. Not Hope.

3.1 Change Your Life?
Change Your Habits.

Assuming today was a normal day, what did you do?

I know the odds are high that what you did today was very similar to what you did the day before. *And* the day before that. And ... you get it.

Your alarm probably woke you up, just like every normal day.

You went to the bathroom to get rid of liquid. Then went to the kitchen to fill up with liquid. (*Caffeinated* liquid.) You may have checked your email or scrolled through social media while you waited for your coffee. If that's what you did today, I bet that's what you did yesterday.

After that you might have worked out or read your Bible or eaten breakfast or turned on the news or done some combination of those things. Whatever you did, it was probably what you always do.

Then you took a shower. (Or maybe not. If you didn't, put "bathing" high on your to-do list for tomorrow!)

You did indistinguishable tasks at your job and sat through indistinguishable meetings with indistinguishable people.

Your job was interrupted midday by lunch. My hunch is you don't deviate much on what you munch for lunch. You bring one of a couple of "regular" options from home or head out to one of a few favorite restaurants.[23]

If you commute to work, the scary thing is that you may not remember driving home. *Wait! How did I get here?* You have developed the ability to drive from work to your house on autopilot. (Why is that not considered a superpower?)

At home, you ordered takeout or you cooked dinner. (And then griped that no one helped you cook. And why were you also the one cleaning up the dishes?) Whichever it was—takeout or home cooking—I'm guessing it's what you almost always go for.

After eating, you probably fell into your evening routine. It might be giving the kids their baths. Or making them do their homework. Or scrolling through social media. Or bingeing the next episodes of the TV show you're watching. You might pray or journal.

You may have made a move on your spouse and hoped for the best. Again.

Whatever you did, chances are it was pretty much what you did yesterday and what you'll do tomorrow.

But the sameness of your routine is the same as the sameness of everyone's routines, including mine. Much of what we do is not the result of conscious choices but daily habits. Duke University did a study and found that 40 percent of the actions people take in any given day are the result not of decisions but of habits.[24] Autopilot is not just for people flying airplanes or driving Teslas. We do much of what we do because it's what we always do.

> **Your choices create the course and contours of your life. Your decisions determine your destiny.**

Your choices create the course and contours of your life. Your decisions determine your destiny. And your choices are less intentional and more habitual than you realize.

There's a lot of truth to the quote some attribute to Aristotle, "We are what we repeatedly do."[25] That means:

- Who you are today has been largely shaped by your habits.
- Where you are today has been largely shaped by your habits.
- The life you're living today has been largely shaped by your habits.

If we're honest, our strategy for change is often based on and fueled by hope. "I hope I get the promotion." "I hope my kids start to love God more." "I hope our marriage can improve." But hope is not a strategy.

What got us here is not hope. We are largely who and where we are because of our habits. We need to master the habits that matter most. This means:

- If you want to change who you're becoming, change your habits.
- If you want to change where you're going, change your habits.
- If you want to change your life, change your habits.

How do you change your habits, you ask? That's a fair question since most of us have tried and failed. I've got good news. Changing your habits is easier than you think.

Exercise 13

To give personal context to what I shared in this chapter, write down the basics of your daily routine. Be sure to write down what you actually do—your routine, your rituals, your habits—not what you wish you did or hope to do. The goal of this exercise is for you to look at your routine because so few people ever stop and evaluate their daily habits.

Morning

Midday

Afternoon

Evening

Principle 13

If you want to change who you're becoming, change your habits.

If you want to change where you're going, change your habits.

If you want to change your life, change your habits.

Since Jesus went through everything you're going through and more, learn to think like him. Think of your sufferings as a weaning from that old sinful habit of always expecting to get your own way. Then you'll be able to live out your days free to pursue what God wants instead of being tyrannized by what you want.

—1 Peter 4:1–2 MSG

3.2 Flossing Saved My Life

Never underestimate how God can start something big through one small habit.

That has been one of the greatest lessons of my life. I'll share some personal examples, including the habit that saved my life—flossing. (No, not the TikTok dance, the actual dental procedure. Context is critical these days.)

First, I want to tell you about Daniel. His life illustrates the power of some life-changing principles:

- Never underestimate how God can start something big through one small habit.
- The small things no one sees can lead to the big results everyone wants.
- Success happens not by accident but by habits.

Daniel was a Jew living in Jerusalem. Like you, what he did each new day was probably similar to what he'd done the day before.

I assume he woke up and immediately grabbed his cappuccino, which was already made because of his programmable coffee maker. He

> **Never underestimate how God can start something big through one small habit.**

checked Facebook. Turned on the TV to see the news. Put on his skinny jeans and not-tucked-in button-up shirt for Casual Friday at work. Jumped in his SUV and headed into the city.

Or maybe not. After "he woke up," nothing in that last paragraph is remotely accurate. Daniel lived around 600 BC, before people had personal cappuccino makers and wore joggers.

But it is true that, like everyone else, Daniel had normal days shaped by his daily habits. That is, until the day the Babylonians invaded Jerusalem and took most of the people to Babylon. Daniel was taken and forced to live in captivity.

A horrible experience, until:

The Babylonian king, Nebuchadnezzar, chose the most promising young people from all the captives. Daniel was one of those chosen in Nebby's "30 under 30" group. The king wanted to indoctrinate these good-looking, bright, impressive future leaders so they could be trained to serve him. Because of his faithfulness to God, Daniel refused to follow some of the king's training regimen. But Daniel did it in such a way that he didn't lose anyone's respect. Eventually, he won the king over with his phenomenal insight and wisdom: "Then King Nebuchadnezzar fell prostrate before Daniel and paid him honor and ordered that an offering and incense be presented to him. The king said to Daniel, 'Surely your God is the God of gods and the Lord of kings and a revealer of mysteries, for you were able to reveal this mystery.' Then the king placed Daniel in a high position and lavished many gifts on him" (Dan. 2:46–48).

Later, Daniel's actions led the king to put his faith in God—at least in the moment: "Now I, Nebuchadnezzar, praise and exalt and glorify the King of heaven, because everything he does is right and all his ways are just" (Dan. 4:37).

Eventually Nebuchadnezzar died, and his son Belshazzar became the new king. Belshazzar was not really aware of Daniel. (Apparently, he didn't follow Daniel on Instagram.) But he encountered a problem no one could solve, and someone told him to bring in Daniel.

Daniel showed up and offered knowledge and understanding,

giving the king the answer he needed: "Then at Belshazzar's command, Daniel was clothed in purple, a gold chain was placed around his neck, and he was proclaimed the third highest ruler in the kingdom" (Dan. 5:29).

Belshazzar died, and Darius took over as king. Darius chose 120 of the most impressive young people in the country to enter into a leadership training program. Daniel was once again selected as a future mover and shaker. That alone is amazing, but soon Daniel set himself apart from the other 119: "Now Daniel so distinguished himself among the administrators and the satraps by his exceptional qualities that the king planned to set him over the whole kingdom" (Dan. 6:3).

We hope to live the kind of life Daniel lived. He was repeatedly chosen and promoted. He consistently influenced people for God in amazing ways.

As you might imagine, some people did not appreciate all of Daniel's success. Jealous of how he kept being promoted, they planned to take him down. But these enemies could not find a single flaw or weakness in Daniel. Desperate to accuse him of something, anything, they realized the only way they could trip him up was by attacking his faith in God.

So they tricked the king into issuing a decree they knew Daniel would not obey. The law stated that a person who prayed to anyone other than the king would be thrown into a den of lions.

How did Daniel respond to the king outlawing prayer? "When Daniel learned that the law had been signed, he went home and knelt down as usual in his upstairs room, with its windows open toward Jerusalem. He prayed three times a day, just as he had always done, giving thanks to his God" (Dan. 6:10 NLT).

Did you notice the "as usual" and "three times a day" and "just as he had always done"? Daniel had a prayer habit. And that habit made all the difference in every area of his life.

Daniel always stood out. He was taken prisoner from his country by an evil nation but ended up leading and transforming that evil nation. People saw God in his life and turned to God because of him. When he was thrown into the lions' den for praying, he (spoiler alert) faced down the lions.

We see that and think, *Whaaaa? He was so lucky! I hope I can have that kind of life someday.*

No. It was not luck. And God didn't make Daniel some sort of superhero, different from you and me.

A habit shaped Daniel's identity, giving him the confidence to be who God created him to be and do what God called him to do.

Daniel's habit was praying. Not once a day. Not twice a day. *Three* times a day. He did not pray only when it was convenient or easy. He didn't just pray when he was in trouble. Or when he was done watching all the good shows on Amazon Prime and had nothing better to do.

He prayed every day.

Three times a day.

Daniel may not have considered praying three times a day a big deal. You might wonder why his practice of praying led to a nation-changing impact and having a book of the Bible dedicated to his life. Never underestimate how God can start something big through one small habit.

Daniel's success happened not by accident but by habits.

You may wonder whether this was just a Daniel thing. It's not. When you see someone who has something you want—financial freedom, a happy marriage, great physical fitness, intimacy with God, influence in the world—then you can feel confident that success did not happen by accident. It happened by habits. Their winning is not the result of luck. Not the result of a moment. It didn't happen because of one big, bold action or decision. Their winning is the result of doing the right strategic habits, over and over, day after day.

The small things no one sees can lead to the big results everyone wants.

Hope doesn't change your life. Habits do. Specifically, mastering the habits that matter most.

That is good news. Why?

> **The small things no one sees can lead to the big results everyone wants.**

- Because you are not a victim of circumstances.
- Because you don't need something big to magically happen. If you want something big to happen, start small.
- Because you don't have to keep helplessly hoping for change. You can start and maintain habits that will lead to change.

This truth has made all the difference in my life and leadership. For more than three decades, I have started one new habit a year. Most have been small and seemingly insignificant. If you looked over the thirty-plus years, you would see I had a few years where my new habit didn't take. I also have intentionally dropped a few habits along the way. But I can tell you with confidence that I have started more than twenty new habits that are now a consistent part of my life.

I couldn't point to any one of those habits and say, "That's what made me close to God, a great husband to Amy, a good dad to my kids, and an effective leader." But together, these habits have reshaped how I see myself and how I treat people. They have renewed my mind and revived my spiritual confidence. They have changed my body and my posture. My life is transformed, and it happened one small habit at a time.

Here are a few examples.

The first habit I established was flossing. (To remind you, not the dance move. But that may be my new habit for next year. Or the Whip. Or the Dougie.) The first daily discipline I committed to was flossing my teeth. Why? Because I hate flossing my teeth. I needed to start flossing my teeth to convince myself that I am a person who chooses what's right over what's convenient. As odd as that sounds, flossing helped introduce and establish my identity as a disciplined person. From that foundation, I began adding one new strategic habit a year.

When I first became a Christian, I desperately wanted to be close to God. I knew no one just stumbles into intimacy with God. *How did this happen? I was just sitting here playing Candy Crush and now I'm tight with Jesus and full of spiritual strength! Whoa!* Hoping would not grow my relationship with God. Habits would. So I committed to the discipline of tithing. Anytime God blesses me with a financial increase, I put him first by giving back at least 10 percent.

Over the years, tithing has been a constant reminder that God is my provider and the source of all the good things in my life. (What we so often think is about money is never actually about money. Tithing is no exception.)

When Amy and I were dating we decided we would worship God every week at church. We have. I promise there has never been one conversation in my house where someone asked, "Are we going to church this weekend?" My kids will tell you we usually find a church to attend even when we're on vacation. Why? It's who we are—the people of God. And it's who we want to become—people who always put God first.

Another early habit came because I knew God's Word contained the truth that would set me free. So I resolved to read the Bible every day. (If you are feeling a little guilty because you don't, please note: the fact that I decided to do it means there was a time when I didn't.) I started reading the Bible daily. One year, I made up my mind to read it from cover to cover. I've now read the Bible from front to back every year for about two decades. My habit of reading the Bible every day turned into a habit of reading all of the Bible every year.

One year, I chose daily journaling as my new habit. But I failed. I started again another year. I failed again. Then I found a five-year journal where you journal only five lines a day. That worked for me. Every day since, I have recorded five lines of what God is doing in my life. If there's a day I want to write more, great, but the habit is five lines a day.

I didn't used to pray with my wife. There were several reasons. One was that Amy takes about forty-five minutes to get warmed up. Don't tell her I said this, but I'd feel like, *Get on with it, Amy.* (I'm pretty sure God, too, was like, *Get on with it, Amy.*) Another reason was that I was lazy. So we didn't pray together, but we knew we should.

One year we established a new habit: before I leave for work, we join hands and pray a short prayer. (Amy can pray for another forty-four minutes after I leave if she wants.) Every day we connect with God together. Though it's short, it's powerful. We figured out how to establish the habit in a way that worked for both of us.

One year, I became increasingly aware of some wrong thinking and personal insecurities. I wrote a list of declarations, based on God's truth, that countered the lies I was tempted to believe. (You can see these declarations and learn how to develop your own in my book *Winning the War in Your Mind*.) I established a new habit of reading those declarations out loud every day.

Some years I chose health-related habits. I used to drink more Dr Pepper and Mountain Dew than a speedway full of NASCAR fans on a hot Texas Saturday. One year, I determined to quit drinking soda and drink only water. Another year, I chose to limit myself to one dessert a week.

I could tell you more, but it all goes back to the one habit I believe made all my habits possible—flossing. In his book *The Power of*

Habit, Charles Duhigg writes about a "keystone habit." He describes how certain habits propel you to establish other habits.[26] I believe Daniel praying three times a day was a keystone habit. Daily prayer created momentum for other God-honoring disciplines and helped him become who he was supposed to become.

My keystone habit was flossing. That may sound silly. But when I floss, I tell myself I'm disciplined. Therefore, because I'm disciplined, I go to bed on time, get up on time, do my Bible reading plan, go to work, have a productive day, work out, come home in a good mood, and kiss my wife, which is why we have six kids. (Can I get an amen?)

If I don't floss, I don't feel disciplined. Therefore, since I don't feel disciplined, I stay up too late at night, hit snooze in the morning, don't have time to do my Bible plan, rush to work, am not productive, so I have a bad day, stay late, and don't work out. I know Amy will be mad at me, so I speed home, a police officer tries to pull me over, and I don't want a ticket, so I try to outrun them, and, after a long car chase, I am eventually captured and put in jail. Why? Because I didn't floss!

I'm obviously exaggerating, but the reality for me is that flossing has changed my life. Flossing was the first domino that started a chain reaction of thirty years of creating habits. Like I said, some years were not as successful, but overall, the discipline of habits began, and the habit of discipline began.

Remember, you do what you do because of what you think of you. I used to think I was not a disciplined person. There was plenty of evidence to substantiate that belief. Flossing proved to me that I am disciplined.

You are disciplined too. There are many things you do every single day. Habits you have established. Because you are disciplined. You currently may have the wrong habits. But you can change that. For now, realize you are disciplined and have been establishing new habits your whole life.

We're now going to:

1. Get intentional with what habits we want to start.
2. Get intentional with what habits we need to stop.

Choosing the right habits will change your life. In fact, that's exactly how you change your life. Habits, not hope. Change your habits. Change your life.

So what's your flossing? Your first domino? Your gateway habit toward change?

I'm going to encourage you to choose one small habit that will be easy to start. Small? Easy? Yep. But never underestimate how God can start something big through one small habit. And remember: the small things no one sees can lead to the big results everyone wants.

Exercise 14

Because we're talking about mastering the habits that matter most, what is the first habit you can establish that could lead to your biggest win? Take a look back at my examples in this chapter, if needed.

Principle 14

**Never underestimate how God can start
something big through one small habit.**

**The small things no one sees can lead to
the big results everyone wants.**

Success happens not by accident but by habits.

If you are faithful in little things, you will be
faithful in large ones.

—Luke 16:10 NLT

3.3 The Loop

I want to tell you about Sadie. I've known her for years. She's fairly short and has brown hair. Sadie's always impressed me with her intelligence and positive attitude. Unfortunately, she keeps pooping in our yard.

Sadie is our family dog. (Perhaps I should have led with that.) She is smart and loves routine. Whenever I get the garbage can and start to walk it down our long driveway, she bounces up and down with excitement. She then leads the way to scare off any predators. (At least that's what I think she thinks she's doing.)

When I take her out the back door, she immediately sits down on the porch and waits to be brushed. Since our yard isn't fenced, I used to put her on a leash to walk her to our small dog pen. But now, all I have to do is show her the leash, and she dashes full speed to her dog pen, lies down, and waits for me to close the door.

Sadie follows predictable routines based on visual cues.

We tend to do the same thing. Like Sadie, we are creatures of habit. We respond to simple cues.

And if we're going to start healthy habits and stop hurtful ones, we need to first make sure we understand how habits work.

What Is a Habit?

A habit is basically behavioral autopilot.

Habits work with the way your brain works. Your brain is wired to conserve energy, wanting things to be easy. That's why your brain loves habits. Habits allow you to act without thinking. A habit allows good or bad behavior to happen without your brain having to take charge. (Just like for Sadie the garbage can means a walk down the driveway, the back door means getting brushed, and the leash means getting into the dog pen.)

We do things without having to think about them. We do things without having to decide to do them. Like brushing your teeth. When you brush your teeth, you're not thinking, *Hmmm. I'm going to push this toothbrush up. Yes! That worked! Now down? Yes, down. And maybe up again? Uh huh, I think so. And down. Now let's change it up. Push right! Left!* No. You brush your teeth on behavioral autopilot. You don't think about it, you just do it.

> **A habit allows good or bad behavior to happen without your brain having to take charge.**

A habit is a behavior you automatically fall into without your brain fully participating in the decision-making.

How Are Habits Born?

Most experts say we establish habits through a three-step loop:

1. Cue
2. Response
3. Reward

Personally, I like the fourth one that James Clear adds:

1. Cue
2. Craving
3. Response
4. Reward[27]

The *cue* is a trigger that alerts your brain to go into autopilot by engaging the habit.

The *craving* is the physical, mental, or emotional need the cue leads you to want to satisfy.

The *response* is the behavior you routinely fall into.

The *reward* is how the behavior makes you feel.

If the behavior creates pleasure, your brain decides this is a loop worth remembering for the future.[28] The next time the cue appears, your brain tells you, "Hey! Dummy! I know a way we can feel good right now!" and will lead you to the behavior that worked last time. If you engage in the same loop—cue, craving, response, reward—enough times, the process will become automatic. The cue will create a powerful sense of anticipation. The cue and reward will become intertwined. A habit will be born.

> If you engage in the same loop—cue, craving, response, reward—enough times, the process will become automatic.

Here are some examples of bad habit loops:

- Cue: a few minutes of idle time
  - Craving: entertainment
  - Response: pull up social media on your phone
  - Reward: dopamine rush to the brain
- Cue: a hard day at work
  - Craving: stress relief
  - Response: drink alcohol
  - Reward: escape thinking about your jerk boss
- Cue: driving past a fast-food joint on the way home
  - Craving: greasy comfort food
  - Response: get food in the drive-through and scarf it in your car (the way God intended for us to eat our meals)
  - Reward: another dopamine rush that feels good

Get a Clue about Your Cues

To effectively start and stop habits, we need to understand how cues (or triggers) work and identify ours.

Studies show there are five major categories of triggers:

1. PLACE

A place can be the cue that initiates a habit loop. For instance, you may find it is easier to be grateful and focused in prayer when you're in a church building. In contrast, you probably aren't tempted to smoke weed when you're in a church building.

2. TIME

Certain times can trigger behaviors. You might feel inspired to exercise early in the morning. You may tend to worry when you lie in bed at night.

Time and place matter a lot. When we create a plan for establishing new habits and ending old ones, time and place will be essential.

Here's our strategy:

1. We will create time and place triggers to start a good habit.
2. We will remove time and place triggers to stop a bad habit.

3. MOOD

Moods can cue cravings and lead us into behaviors. You may have good moods that trigger good habits. You are also more open to temptation and engaging in unhealthy habits when you are in a bad mood. Experts say we need to HALT when we see a mood coming that makes us vulnerable. HALT is an acronym for hungry, angry, lonely, and tired. If you survey your life and find self-destructive habits, you'll see they often occur when you're hangry (hungry + angry), all by yourself, or exhausted.

4. MOMENTS

The fourth major category of cues is moments. Certain types of moments launch specific habit loops. You get in a fight with your spouse and you immediately find yourself calling a friend to complain. You pass your test in school and get drunk to celebrate. You feel disapproval, so you grab a carton of ice cream and a spoon.

5. PEOPLE

The last type of trigger is people. The bad news? Wrong people can be cues that lead us in the wrong direction. The good news is that right people can trigger right behavior. Studies prove that the closer you get to someone, the more likely it is you'll have the same habits.

In one study, researchers tracked twelve thousand people over thirty-two years. They found people are 57 percent more likely to be overweight if they have a friend who is significantly overweight. Researchers also discovered that when a person loses a substantial amount of weight, one of their three closest friends will as well.[29] The people we hang with shape our habits. God told us that long before studies confirmed it. Proverbs 13:20 says, "Walk with the wise and become wise, for a companion of fools suffers harm," and 1 Corinthians 15:33 says, "Do not be misled: 'Bad company corrupts good character.'"

■ ■ ■

So. Review time.

A habit is basically behavioral autopilot.

A habit is established by repeating a four-step loop: cue, craving, response, reward.

We are wise to understand cues and identify the ones that can trigger our habits.

Got it?

If so, we're ready to start some strategic habits and stop some self-defeating ones.

Exercise 15

Working through the five major triggers/cues, list positives and negatives for each in your life right now. Remember, these are to discover consistent tendencies, not one-off incidents.

PLACES

Places that cue a positive response:

Places that trigger a negative response:

TIMES

Times that cue a positive response:

Times that trigger a negative response:

MOODS

Moods that cue a positive response:

Moods that trigger a negative response:

MOMENTS

Moments that cue a positive response:

Moments that trigger a negative response:

PEOPLE

People who cue a positive response:

People who trigger a negative response:

Principle 15

A habit is basically behavioral autopilot born of the process of cue, craving, response, and reward.

Walk with the wise and become wise;
    associate with fools and get in trouble.

—Proverbs 13:20 NLT

3.4 The Art of the Start

Perhaps you don't have a stellar track record when it comes to establishing new habits. We're going to change that. Based on who you want to become, what is one habit you need to start?

How do you successfully start and maintain a new habit?

First, Make Your Habit Obvious

We tend to do not what's best but what's most obvious. The easiest thing to choose is what's right in front of your face.

So if you want to establish a new habit, make it obvious.

The simplest and most powerful way to do this is visually. You're going to set "action triggers." To change what you do, you need to change what you see.

You want to drink more water? Put your gargantuan water bottle on the counter where you will see it every day.

You want to eat more vegetables? Put those carrots in the front of the fridge so they're the first thing you see when you open the door. You want your carrots greeting you in all their orange glory!

You want to read the Bible every day? Put your Bible on your nightstand. Or choose a YouVersion Bible reading plan online and put the app on your home screen.

This may seem obvious, but most people don't take these simple steps. That's why they struggle to establish new habits.

In their book *Switch: How to Change Things When Change Is*

Hard, Chip Heath and Dan Heath share research on how important it is to "tweak the environment." They write, "Many people have discovered that, when it comes to changing their own behavior, environmental tweaks beat self-control every time." Environmental tweaks? They suggest using a smaller plate if you want to eat less, putting out your sneakers and exercise clothes the night before if you want to jog the next morning, and setting the coffeepot to auto brew at wake-up time so the aroma helps you fight the urge to hit snooze.[30]

Amazing that such a simple effort could make so much of a difference.

> **A small change in what you see can lead to a big shift in what you do.**

A small change in what you see can lead to a big shift in what you do. In *Atomic Habits,* James Clear writes, "You don't have to be the victim of your environment. You can also be the architect of it."[31]

For example, I prioritize taking my supplements first thing in the morning. Taking my supplements gives me a mental edge. They help me work harder *and* smarter, which allows me to get done with my work in time to go to the gym before I go home. Working out makes me feel positive, strong, and healthy. That attitude overflows into my relationship with Amy and my kids.

I need to take my supplements every day! So guess where I put them? Right on the counter where I cannot miss them. Just like those joggers set out their gear the night before. An atomic habit. I am the architect of my environment, and I design it to help me achieve my win.

So you can make your new habit visually obvious by setting action triggers.

You can also make it obvious by preloading your decisions.

Behavioral scientists in Great Britain did another study of

a couple hundred people who wanted to start exercising. They divided the people into three groups. The first group committed to exercising. The second group committed to exercising and reading lots of material on the benefits of exercise. The third group committed to exercising and chose the day, time, and place when they would do it. Only 36 percent of the those in the first two groups kept their commitment. But 91 percent of the people in the third group kept their commitment.[32]

Did you catch that? Barely a third of the people in the first two groups succeeded, but more than nine of ten who committed to a time and place met their goals!

Why? They made their goals obvious by preloading their decisions. Remember, your brain is wired to conserve energy. It doesn't want to think through options. If it has to, it will quit. You don't want your lazy brain to have to work through all that. So decide in advance when and where you will do your new habit.

Experts explain that most people think they lack motivation when what they truly lack is clarity.

Decide in advance. For instance:

- You want to pray more? Great! When and where?
  - "I will pray each morning, after I get my coffee, on my porch, for ten minutes."
- You want to go out on more dates with your spouse? Awesome. When and where?
  - "We will go out for dinner every Friday night as soon as the sitter arrives."
- You want to be a more encouraging person? You could set a visual action trigger by putting a stack of note cards on your desk where you will see them. Then preload when and where.
  - "I will write one card a day to someone first thing after I get to work."

You can make it even more obvious by tying your new habit into something you already do. So create a habit by writing out a declaration that looks like this: I will _____ after I _____.

Daniel prayed three times a day. His declaration might have been, "I will pray after I drink my morning coffee." "I will pray after I eat my sandwich." (Note: For Daniel, it would *not* have been a ham sandwich!)

To start a habit of exercising, you might decide, "After I put my kids to bed, I will do a thirty-second plank."

If you want to read more, you might decide, "After I get into bed, I will read before I go to sleep." To make it even more obvious, put your book on your pillow each morning. That way you'll see it when you are about to get into bed at night.

Habitologists[33] call connecting a new habit to a current habit "habit stacking." It's especially helpful because of the way your brain works. Your brain builds up connections between neurons that are used frequently. Your brain removes connections between neurons that are not used. (That process is sometimes called "synaptic pruning.") Those removed or "pruned" connections are why it's so difficult to remember something you rarely do and so challenging to start doing it. Your built-up connections are why it's so easy for you to remember to do things you frequently do and to do those things.

For instance, perhaps you've made coffee every morning for years. It's easy to do, and you don't forget to do it. Let's say you've never really read the Bible. But now you want to every morning. It will feel challenging to do and will be easy to forget. So connect your new habit of reading the Bible with your established habit of making and drinking coffee. "I will read the Bible while I drink my coffee."

One of the ways I've established new disciplines over the years is to stack one on top of another. For instance, this is my morning routine:

1. My alarm goes off, waking me up.
2. I go to the bathroom. (Not a chosen habit, but you gotta do what you gotta do.)
3. After going to the bathroom, I do my Bible plan.
4. After doing my Bible plan, I pray.
5. After praying, I read my daily declarations.
6. After reading my daily declarations, I make my oatmeal and put twelve berries in it. (Some days I go crazy and do up to fifteen!)
7. After eating my oatmeal (and berries), I take my supplements.
8. After the supplements, I take a shower.
9. After my shower, I shave.
10. After I shave, I get dressed.
11. After I get dressed, I pray with Amy.
12. After I pray with Amy, I leave for work.

Notice how my spiritual growth habits—Bible reading, praying, declarations, praying with my wife—are woven into my morning "get ready" routine. Almost every activity in my morning routine are habits that, at one time, I did not do. But then I decided to start doing them. I was able to establish the habits by making them obvious and stacking them on other habits I was already doing.

How do you successfully start and maintain a new habit? First, make your habit obvious.

Second, Make Your Habit Attractive

The reason you do most of what you do is because it feels good. The behavior makes your brain release dopamine—the "feel good" hormone. That's why it's hard not to do the things you keep doing. You become addicted to that dopamine hit.

So how can you get that working for you?

You make whatever you want to start doing attractive. The more pleasurable you can make it, the more likely you'll keep doing it.

If you want to exercise but hate jogging, that probably isn't what you should choose. What exercise sounds most enjoyable? Lifting weights at the gym? Playing pickleball? Riding a bike? Doing push-ups and sit-ups? Chasing a chicken around your back yard with the *Rocky* soundtrack blaring from your boom box? You are more likely to do your habit if you don't hate doing your habit. So make your habit attractive.

> **You are more likely to do your habit if you don't hate doing your habit.**

Let's say your win is to get closer to God. You decide the strategic habit to get you there is to have a time of praying and reading the Bible every day. By the way, I believe these are essential habits for *everyone*.

Jesus said, "I am the vine; you are the branches. If you remain in me and I in you, you will bear much fruit; apart from me you can do nothing" (John 15:5).

To bear spiritual fruit, Jesus said we need to stay connected with him, stay in communication with him, and be intimate with him. If you do, your life will be productive. You will grow. But if you are not connected, not communicating, not intimate—nothing. You will lack fruitfulness and productivity. I have found that to be absolutely true in my life.

We also follow his lead in getting close to God. Mark 1:35 gives away one of Jesus' obvious habits: "Very early in the morning, while it was still dark, Jesus got up, left the house and went off to a solitary place, where he prayed."

So to establish a daily habit of praying and reading the Bible, you will:

- Make it obvious
- Set a visual action trigger
- Decide when
- Stack the new habit with an established habit
- Decide where you are going to pray and read
- Make your habit attractive

Make it so you don't want to miss it.

To do that you might do the habit sitting in your favorite chair, facing your window with the best view, drinking the most delicious coffee you can afford. You could play some worship music if you love that. Or write out your prayers in a journal if that sounds enjoyable. Or use different color highlighters to mark important words or verses in the Bible if that sounds fun. If you hate music or journaling, or if you think color highlighters are made in a factory in hell, then don't do these things.

Whatever new habit you want to form, make it attractive.

Third, Make Your Habit Easy

Warning: we are about to get weird. (As if we haven't already, but I'm about to blow your mind.)

Remember, your brain considers energy precious and is wired to conserve. If something looks difficult and challenging, your brain is likely to opt out.

That's taking the "path of least resistance." With our behaviors and habits, it's often called the "law of least effort." Basically, when faced with options, your brain wants you to do the one that will take the least work. You don't want to be in a battle royale with your brain, so make your habit easy. That way you'll be more likely to do it even when you don't feel like it.

In fact—this is the blow-your-mind part—experts tell us that when you start a new habit, it should take *less than two minutes* to do.[34]

Seriously? Yep.

So they would say that instead of trying to start the habit "Read before bed," your new habit should be "Read one page before bed." Instead of "Run three miles," your new habit should be "Run for two minutes."

Perhaps you and your spouse have always wanted to pray together. You've tried, but it felt awkward, so you stopped.

How do you start the habit? Make it easy. Create a habit of thanking God together for one thing every day. Just one thing. Grab each other's hands and then each of you thank God for one blessing. "God, thank you that my meeting went well today." "God, thank you that the kids all went down easy at bedtime tonight." That's it.

Starting out, make your habits take less than two minutes to do. You'll discover that once you start doing the right thing, it's much easier to continue doing the right thing. But if you make your habit hard to start, you probably won't. Or you'll start but be tempted to quit. (Let's not even mention that calorie-counting app you downloaded. Remember that?)

The point is not just to do that one thing.

The point is to show up. To start.

Because a minute of reading every day is better than never picking up a book. One push-up each day is better than not exercising at all. A two-minute heart-to-heart with your kid is better than no heart-to-heart.

Better to do less than you were hoping than to do nothing at all. And that small start could take you somewhere really big. I love Zechariah 4:10: "Do not despise these small beginnings, for the LORD rejoices to see the work begin" (NLT).

How do you start and maintain a new habit?

Make it obvious, attractive, and easy.

Fourth, Make Your Habit Communal

Don't do it by yourself. Surround yourself with support—with people who already do what you want to do. That's especially helpful.

All kinds of groundbreaking studies prove the power of other people's influence on our habits. The study I mentioned in the previous chapter found that if a person in a relationship loses a lot of weight, one of their three closest friends will also lose weight. That happens even if the friend doesn't have the same goal and isn't attempting to lose weight.

This explains why the most effective way to overcome an addiction is to join a twelve-step program. These programs are not just about the steps. (Which, by the way, are habits.) They're about joining a group of people with the same struggle and the same goal.

You may have heard the expression that you are the average of the five people with whom you spend the most time. I don't know whether that is scientifically proven, but I'm not taking my chances. If you check out my five closest friends, you will find they all love Jesus. They are all faithfully involved in church. All five are professionals succeeding at their work. They are intentional about what they eat and work out consistently. They live beneath their means financially. They are incredibly generous. It's not random that I've chosen those people as my closest friends. They make it easier for me to live out healthy, God-honoring habits.

Let's say we flipped my script. What if my five closest friends were all unemployed, played video games all day, and struggled with addictions? What if they drank a lot, smoked who knows what, and scarfed down Flamin' Hot Cheetos by the bag? What if they didn't believe in God and thought prayer was stupid? Can you imagine how much more difficult it would be for me to be disciplined and please God?

Living the right life is almost impossible if you have the wrong friends. Of course, you should be close to some people who are far from God. You're called to shine the light of Jesus to them.

> Living the right life is almost impossible if you have the wrong friends.

But you will become most like the people with whom you spend the most time.

Want to build better habits? Join a community where your desired behavior is the normal behavior. While your old way of life seems acceptable when you witness others doing it, new habits seem achievable when you see others doing them.

Fifth, Make Your Habit Repetitious

I am going to try to impress you with a big word.

I hope you're sitting down.

Are you ready? Here it is:

Pneumonoultramicroscopicsilicovolcanoconiosis.

That is actually not the big word I want to teach you, but it is currently the longest word in the English language. It's a lung disease. Apparently, you get it from inhaling silica dust. I guess volcanos produce silica dust. So hold your breath around volcanos? I don't know. I told you, that's not the big word. This is: potentiation.

Huh?

It's the word neuroscientists use to explain how the connections in your brain strengthen based on repeated activity.

Translated from nerd speak: the more you do something, the easier it is to do.

Those brainy brain scientists call it Hebb's rule, which states that neurons that fire together wire together.

That's why when you first start something, it feels awkward, difficult, and no fun. But if you keep doing it, it will eventually feel comfortable, natural, and easy. Even fun, maybe?

Remember the first time you rode a skateboard? Played *Guitar Hero*? Juggled? Wrote computer code? Built a birdhouse? You struggled and wondered whether it was even possible. But if you kept doing it, you mastered it.

The same will be true with whatever habit you're trying to establish. The more you do it, the easier it will be to keep doing it.

Before we wrap up this chapter, let's review. Make your habit:

1. Obvious
2. Attractive
3. Easy
4. Communal
5. Repetitious

This brings us to the question many ask: "If I use these five guides, how long will it take to build a new habit?" Answer? It's not about the number of days but about the number of repetitions. It's not about twenty-one days or thirty days or ninety days. What matters is how many times you do the new behavior. The more often you do it, the more it will become hardwired into your brain, which will make the behavior easier to keep doing.

With repetition, that new habit will go from being hard to start to hard to stop.

> With repetition, that new habit will go from being hard to start to hard to stop.

Speaking of stopping a habit, that's where we're headed next. Because to move toward your win, you probably need to start a new habit or two and stop an old habit or two.

Exercise 16

What is one habit you need to start?

For any change you desire to make, any habit you want to form, any win you want to achieve, personalize the five guides. Look back at my examples if needed.

To help make my habit more obvious, I will _____ after I _____.

To make my habit attractive, I can:

To make my habit easy, I can begin by doing _____for two minutes.

To make my habit communal, I can invite, involve, or join:

To make my habit repetitious, I can:

Principle 16

Make your habit:

1. Obvious
2. Attractive
3. Easy
4. Communal
5. Repetitious

Do not despise these small beginnings, for the LORD rejoices to see the work begin.

—Zechariah 4:10 NLT

3.5 How to Stop before You Flop

Have you noticed how people can summarize years of bad decisions with only one sentence? Someone will shake their head sadly and say, "Yeah, she fell into sin." Or, "He cheated on his wife." Or, "He died of a heart attack at fifty-eight." Or, "She got fired from her dream job."

We can talk like the person had one catastrophically bad day or made one disastrous decision. But people don't ruin their lives by taking one big tragic step. No. It's never one; more like 56,250. (Remember that number.)

There are a bunch of these "life summary sentences" in the Bible. One of the most profound is in Judges 16:1, which summarizes the life of Samson.

If there was ever a guy born with unbelievable potential, it was Samson. God set him apart and gifted him to play an important role. Samson could have been a revered hero of the faith.[35]

But here is his summary sentence, "One day Samson went to the Philistine town of Gaza and spent the night with a prostitute" (NLT). That sentence encapsulates the beginning of Samson's downward trajectory.

There were several reasons why entering Gaza could ruin Samson's life. Gaza was not only a city where Samson could find a prostitute but also the headquarters for the Philistines, who hated God's people. Samson was their public enemy number one.

The statement "One day Samson went to the Philistine town

of Gaza and spent the night with a prostitute" reads like an abrupt choice. Like Samson woke up with nothing to do one Sunday. It wasn't football season, so there were no games on TV. He checked Netflix but couldn't find a show to watch. He thought about riding his Peloton but wasn't in the mood. Then Samson had an idea. *This has never occurred to me before, but I'm pretty sure there are prostitutes in Gaza. I think I'll just head over there today.*

No. Disasters are rarely the result of an isolated decision. They are almost always the end of a slippery slope. Far more earth is moved every day by erosion than landslides. But no one notices erosion, just landslides. Choices are no different.

> **Disasters are rarely the result of an isolated decision.**

I did a little geography research on this passage. Samson lived in the town of Zorah, some say twenty-five miles from Gaza. Since Uber was still a few (thousand) years from its start-up, we can assume Samson probably walked to Gaza. Do you know how many steps it takes to go twenty-five miles? Approximately 56,250. (And you thought that number from earlier was random, didn't you?)

Samson did not ruin his life all at one time. He took 56,250 steps in a direction that began a downward, out-of-control spiral. Long before he headed to Gaza that day, Samson must have allowed 56,250 thoughts, little decisions, and self-defeating habits to deteriorate his relationship with God and his own integrity. This led him to a weakened place where he was willing to do something outside of God's will.

If you read the rest of Samson's story, you'll see he continued to make a series of small, bad decisions and engage in compromising habits that led him, step by step, to ruin his life.

Who does that?

We all do.

Well, we all can. We don't wreck our lives all at once but a little at a time. Like erosion. We're all tempted to slide down that 56,250-step slope every day.

That's why it's so important to get hold of our habits. You've thought about who you want to become, and we've asked what one habit you need to start.

Here's our next challenge: based on who you want to become, what one habit do you need to stop?

What unhealthy, unhelpful, and perhaps ungodly habit is taking you in a direction you don't want to go? You don't *need* to go?

In his letter to the Colossians, Paul writes about your true you and who you want to become: "You have been raised to life with Christ. Now set your heart on what is in heaven, where Christ rules at God's right side. Think about what is up there, not about what is here on earth. You died, which means that your life is hidden with Christ, who sits beside God. . . . Each of you is now a new person. You are becoming more and more like your Creator, and you will understand him better" (Col. 3:1–3, 10 CEV).

Paul encourages us: Forget about who you were. Know who you are in Christ and who you want to become in him.

How do you do that? Paul continues: "Don't be controlled by your body. Kill every desire for the wrong kind of sex. Don't be immoral or indecent or have evil thoughts. Don't be greedy, which is the same as worshiping idols. . . . You must quit being angry, hateful, and evil. You must no longer say insulting or cruel things about others. And stop lying to each other. You have given up your old way of life with its habits" (Col. 3:5, 8–9 CEV).

As always, Paul is clear: if you want to become who you want to become, there are some habits you need to give up.

So based on who you want to become, what one habit do you need to break? I know twenty-seven probably come to mind. (I know that because twenty-seven come to *my* mind.) If you try to stop doing twenty-seven things, you will stop doing zero. The Accuser knows that if he can keep you focused on and overwhelmed by all those issues, he'll keep defeating you. So how many of those twenty-seven do you think God wants you to focus on? One. One at a time.

So let's focus on just one habit you want to break.

It might be complaining and being negative. Or gossiping. (That includes sharing "prayer requests" about other people. "Pray for John. I saw on Facebook that he's involved in . . ." "Pray for Jane. I heard from two people at church that she's struggling with . . .")

Maybe you struggle with an eating disorder—purging or bingeing. You may need to stop playing video games. Or watching Netflix. Or porn. You may be addicted to a substance like nicotine or prescription meds. Or biting your fingernails. Or biting a *stranger*'s fingernails!

What is the one habit you need to stop?

A habit I chose to break was engaging in too much screen time. My close friend Apple started informing me how many hours I looked at my phone each week. Honestly, the first time I saw the notification, the number horrified me. I shared it with a few other people who told me it was "less than average." But that didn't make me feel better.

God has given me one life to live for him, and I don't want to waste a bunch of time staring at a screen. So I set limits on apps and took some other measures to decrease my screen time.

You cannot defeat what you cannot define.

Based on who you want to become, what is the one habit you need to break? Once you name it, you can work on stopping. You cannot defeat what you cannot define.

Let me say that one more time: you cannot defeat what you cannot define.

■ ■ ■

Now that you've chosen the habit, how will you stop?

You know it's difficult. You've tried to break bad habits before.

But why is it so challenging?

One reason we struggle to stop doing what we want to stop doing is timing. It's the flip side of why we struggle to start new habits: Good habits are difficult to start because the pain comes now and the payoff is in the future. Bad habits are difficult to stop because the payoff comes now and the pain is in the future.

For example, let's say you want to start jogging. You get excited, thinking, *Yes! I am a jogger! I'm going to jog every day. I'll get in great shape. I'll lose weight!* So the next morning your alarm goes off. *Argh. It is so early!* But you get up and put on your exercise clothes and sneakers. *What am I doing up this early?* You go outside and it's cold! *What the heck? Why is it so cold so early in the morning?*

You start jogging, and before long, your legs hurt, your feet hurt, even your thumbs hurt. *Why do my thumbs hurt? Everything hurts!* You quickly went from excited to exhausted. After a few days of that, you check the scale. *Wait. I've lost only one pound? How is that even possible? Is it worth it to do all this to lose just one pound?*

Good habits are difficult to start because the pain comes now and the payoff is in the future. If you keep jogging consistently, you will see results. You'll lose ten pounds. You'll have buns of steel. Like the groundhog in Punxsutawney, your abs may peek out from where they've been hibernating. All of that will happen—but later. When it does, it will be totally worth it. The hassle, the early, the cold, the thumb pain, all of it. But getting from now to later can feel like hard, monotonous, unrewarding work.

If you try to stop a bad habit, you will experience the exact opposite. Why? Because the bad habit is offering you an immediate perceived benefit. Doing what's wrong can be enjoyable. That sounds like something we shouldn't admit, like saying, "Sin can be fun." Guess what? It can. It is! If you don't think sin can be fun, you aren't doing it right. If doing wrong was never enjoyable, we would never do it. It's fun now but messes you up later.

For example, let's say you get inspired one Sunday to shut off your social media. *Yes! I have new life in Christ, and I am becoming more and more like him! No more endless scrolling, comparing, looking, lusting, and liking!*

Then Monday arrives. You have some free time. You're bored and trying to come up with something to do. You check your phone. The apps are still there. That's when you remember: *Wait. Scrolling and looking feels good.* You tell yourself, *No. I decided yesterday that I don't want to look at any socials anymore.* But you are really bored. And the dopamine rush would feel really good.

You second-guess yourself. *Did I really say never? I'm not sure that's even possible. What am I gonna do instead? Am I really going to play stupid games on my phone when I could . . . I mean, I've done it so many times. What would it matter if I looked one more time? What if I miss something important? I guess I could just do it today and then stop after that. Or maybe on the first of next month. Then I'll have an official stop date that will be easy to remember!*

Why do you convince yourself to do what you don't want to do? Because doing it feels good—*now.*

Bad habits are difficult to stop because the payoff comes now and the pain is in the future. If you don't stop, you will never feel free. You will never feel victory. You'll continue to experience distractions and guilt that get in the way of intimacy with God and potentially get in the way of your relationship with your spouse or future spouse, kids, and others.

Stopping a habit now could prevent a secret from being exposed. If you don't want people finding out, or if you don't want to risk being embarrassed and ashamed or losing the respect of those you love, or if you don't want to forfeit something you treasure, like a position or influence on people, all of that *will* happen—later. When it does, you'd do anything to go back and stop that habit now. Well, you are at now, *now*. You *can* stop now.

But to stop, to avoid that pain later, you're going to have to experience the pain of saying no to pleasure now. This moment might be the entire reason you're reading this book. For you right now, it's not about something you need to start but about dealing with something that could destroy you sooner than later if you don't stop.

■ ■ ■

I think we're finally ready to stop. We know the bad habit we need to break to become who we want to become. How do we do it?

Remember how we start new good habits? We make them obvious and easy. To stop old bad habits, we're going to make them difficult.

I love the way Solomon says the same thing, six different ways, in two short sentences: "Do not set foot on the path of the wicked or walk in the way of evildoers. Avoid it, do not travel on it; turn from it and go on your way" (Prov. 4:14–15).

Here's my paraphrase of Solomon's idea: Why resist a temptation tomorrow if you have the power to eliminate it today?

Instead of hoping to defeat the temptation with willpower and motivation, we will do everything possible not to face the temptation at all. And when we do have to face the temptation, we'll make it as difficult as possible to say yes.

> Why resist a temptation tomorrow if you have the power to eliminate it today?

How are we going to do that?

Remember the habit loop starts with a cue. The cue triggers a craving, which leads you to respond. That action is followed by a reward (the dopamine hit)—some kind of pleasurable feeling.

So how do you break a habit?

You remove the cue.

Previously, I said we need to understand cues and identify the ones that trigger our habits. This is why. We are going to remove the triggers that tempt us to take actions that lead in the wrong direction. If we can't remove a cue altogether, we will put up some roadblocks to prevent us from setting foot on "the path of the wicked."

Let's get really practical with some examples.

Perhaps your battle is with porn. You might be single and justify your porn habit because all your friends are hooking up while you're not. You think of porn as *my one little thing. It's not that big of a deal. I just look.* Or you might be married but justify watching porn because your spouse "isn't meeting your needs." You rationalize what you're doing. But you're racked with guilt and wrecked by shame. You want to stop. You've tried. But now the problem is you don't believe you can.

How do you win that battle and break the habit?

Remove the triggers. God is the one who gave us this idea of eliminating (instead of battling) temptation: "Flee from sexual immorality" (1 Cor. 6:18). "Run from anything that stimulates youthful lusts" (2 Tim. 2:22 NLT).

How might you eliminate porn triggers? Your plan will be based on your clues about your cues. What "stimulates" your "youthful lusts"?

- Scrolling social media?
- Playing computer games when your spouse is asleep?
- Being in a hotel room alone when you're traveling on business?
- Reading a romance novel?
- Watching a certain TV show?
- Seeing ads on webpages for "articles" about cheerleader fails?

Whatever it is, how can you eliminate the temptation?

Personally, I'm not willing to fall to sexual temptation because I could lose everything. So I have put safeguards in my life.

- I am never alone with a woman (who is not family) in *any* context.
- I am not able to download apps.
- I've got adult content blocked.
- Everything is tracked on my computer.
- My settings prevent me from deleting anything.
- I have about six people who have all my passwords so they can look at what I've been viewing or what messages I've sent or received.
- I've got my computer, iPad, and phone locked down. To the best of my knowledge, there is no way to view inappropriate content.

Whatever it is, how can you eliminate the temptation?

You might be thinking, *But Craig, you're a pastor. Are you really that weak and vulnerable?* My answer? No. Not normally. Not most of the time. But you never know when you're going to be in the wrong place at the wrong time in the wrong mood. So why would I resist a temptation tomorrow if I have the power to eliminate it today?

What steps, however radical they might be, can you take to remove your cues? Do you need a friend's help to delete Instagram from your phone? Or even to delete your web browser? Or, if you're smart enough to get around limits, do you need to give up your smart phone for a dumb phone? That would be painful, but your purity is worth it. You don't want to let anything take you out of intimacy with God and intimacy with a person who is real and truly matters to you.

You may be facing a different battle. Whatever habit you want to stop, how can you remove the trigger and make it really difficult to continue doing that habit?

Let's say the habit you want to stop is hitting snooze. You typically hit snooze seven times because, well, isn't that a godly number? How do you stop? Start with who before do. How is hitting snooze keeping you from being who you want to be? Decide that each day is a gift from God that you want to dive into with joy and power. Then eliminate the temptation.

How?

Put your alarm clock, or mobile device, on the other side of the room. Plug it in as far from your bed as you can. That way when it goes off, to hit snooze you have to get out of your warm and snuggly bed and walk across your cold room. And now you're up!

Perhaps you have a problem spending too much on Amazon. Confess your issue to a trusted friend. Then ask that friend to change your password and not tell you the new one. From now on, you can buy something only through that friend. You're making it difficult to do what you don't want to do.

Let me encourage you if you are really deep into a habit: if you have an addiction—perhaps to gambling or alcohol or drugs or sex—it could be time for rehab. Own up to the problem and decide that you won't let it control your life anymore. Seek out a counselor who can point you in the right direction. Don't keep going in the wrong direction. Your God loves you too much. He created you with amazing potential and gave you this one life as a gift. You are worth way too much to waste your life.

Based on who you want to become, what one habit do you need to break?

Remember Samson's 56,250 steps? His "life summary" of "One day Samson went to the Philistine town of Gaza and spent the night with a prostitute"? If you're on a downward spiral like Samson, well, someday people could summarize your life with a statement too. They'll make it sound like your downfall was an isolated decision that defined your life.

But it won't be. The habits you have today are shaping who you will become tomorrow. One step at a time, your habits are taking you somewhere.

If you don't like where they're taking you, change your habits. If you change your habits, you will change your life.

Exercise 17

This exercise is more intensive for good reason. If a habit you are struggling with, especially in secret, could lead to a Samson-type ending for you, digging in and being fully transparent in your response to these questions could bring clarity and understanding. Let your answers lead to change, and let the change lead to freedom.

What is the one habit you know you most need to stop?

What is the best thing that could happen if you are successful and quit?

What is the worst thing that could happen if you continue or get worse?

When you think about stopping, what is your rationalization for continuing?

What cues regularly create triggers for your habit?

Principle 17

Good habits are difficult to start because the pain comes now and the payoff is in the future.

Bad habits are difficult to stop because the payoff comes now and the pain is in the future.

Let's not get tired of doing what is good. At just the right time we will reap a harvest of blessing if we don't give up.

—Galatians 6:9 NLT

3.6 From So to Who

A couple of years ago, I had a big revelation. I'd been working on developing personal discipline for a long time. People who looked at my efforts might have said I'd been successful. Yet I was never satisfied. I was always wanting something else, something more. One day, it hit me: I had the wrong kind of goals. And the wrong kind of goals led me to the wrong motivation for starting and stopping habits.

My goals were primarily *means goals*. My goals were just a means to an end.

How do you know if your goal is a means goal? On the other side of the goal is a *so*.

- "I want to get good grades *so* I can go to a good college, *so* I can get a good job, and *so* I can make lots of money."
- "I want to lose weight *so* I can look better in my clothes, *so* I can attract someone decent to date, and *so* I can get married."

That's a problem. Why? Because if there's a so on the other side, we're training ourselves to defer contentment to the future.

Instead of so goals, I realized I needed to set end goals. I want goals, and habits, that lead to an end. And the only end on the other side of every so is not a what but a who.

Huh? (No, this isn't another one of my weird Dr. Seuss-isms.)

Let me explain. As followers of Christ, we want goals that are not about what we are getting or what we are doing but about who we are becoming. Not getting, not doing, becoming. And the who we want to become more like is Christ. The Colossians 3 passage in the previous chapter said you are becoming more and more like him. That's exactly who we want to become.

> When becoming more like Jesus is the driving force of your life, success is no longer out there somewhere.

When becoming more like Jesus is the driving force of your life, success is no longer out there somewhere. You can be successful today by taking another step toward Christlikeness.

That's the thing about our habits. We think of them as actions. But they are way more than that. Because our habits define our identities.

- I start a new habit of eating right. Why? Because I am becoming more like Jesus. And when I eat right, I am honoring God by being a temple of the Holy Spirit (1 Cor. 6:19–20).
- I start a new habit of waking up earlier. Why? Because I want to create time to read my Bible. Why? Because I am becoming more like Jesus. And reading the Bible renews my mind so I can take my thoughts captive and make them obedient to Christ (2 Cor. 10:5).
- I stop an old habit of looking at porn. Why? Because I am becoming more like Jesus. When I don't lust after images, I can live a pure life of integrity (Col. 3:5–7).

We've said, "If you want to change who you're becoming, change your habits." That is ultimately what we want to do—change who we're becoming.

We've said, "The small things no one sees can lead to the big results everyone wants." The big result we want is to be more like Jesus.

We've said, "Success happens not by accident but by habits."

More than anything else, success is becoming more like Jesus.

So if success happens by habits, what habit do you need to start? What habit do you need to stop so you can become more like Jesus?

As Christ followers, our end goal, our ultimate win, our true mark of success is becoming more like him.

You're about to find out when you do the right strategic habits—consistently—the results will go beyond anything you could imagine.

Exercise 18

To close out this section, consider how you may have made your goals "means goals" (or *so* goals). Use this pattern to change your current and future goals from means goals to end goals.

MY MEANS/SO GOAL

I want to _____
_____*so I can* _____,
so I can _____, *so I can* _____
_____.

MY END GOAL

I want to start a new habit of _____.
Why? Because I am becoming more like Jesus. And when I _____
_____, *I am / I can* _____
_____.

Principle 18

Success is becoming more like Jesus.

Yes, everything else is worthless when compared with the infinite value of knowing Christ Jesus my Lord.

—Philippians 3:8 NLT

Part 4

Sowing. Not Reaping.

4.1 Fanatical Consistency

Do you ever look at really successful people and wonder how they do it? Maybe they are successful in their jobs or marriages. Or with their health or finances. Or perhaps they seem really close to God and have a great impact for him.

How do successful people become successful people?

Growing up, I assumed many of them were just lucky. Lucky to be born into the right family. Lucky to have the right God-given abilities. Lucky to have gotten a big break. Lucky to have met the right person or people. Or maybe they were carrying around the world's most magical rabbit foot. Or a whole stinkin' rabbit.

Then, as I got older, I got to know people who were successful. And I realized I'd been wrong.

Successful people are not lucky. They're consistent.

I mean, sure, perhaps a few successful people have gotten more breaks than most. You can probably think of some business big shots who started with an advantage because of their parents. But if you get to know successful people, you'll realize their success was not serendipitous. It was also not the result of a single moment, like one big, bold action or decision. (Just like we said failure is not a landslide but an erosion. It works both ways.) People succeed. They achieve their win because of countless seemingly small actions and decisions made consistently over time. That consistency gives them the power to change.

Researchers have long attempted to distinguish what separates standout leaders from the rest of the pack. The problem is, when interviewed, leaders often cannot explain the reason for their success. They can identify "no single defining action, no grand program, no one killer innovation, no solitary lucky break, no miracle moment."[36]

So what have the researchers concluded? They've found that "fanatical consistency"[37] leads to the success of the best of the best. These leaders are successful because of their dogged zealousness of doing the same (usually small) right things over and over.

Understanding this revolutionized my life. I believe it can do the same for you.

So are you ready for another principle that flips the script when we apply it to our lives?

Successful people do consistently what other people do occasionally.

What do successful people do consistently? Habits. The right strategic habits. As we've already established: Success happens not by accident but by habits. Successful people start and maintain the right habits and keep doing them.

> **Successful people do consistently what other people do occasionally.**

Some people occasionally put a little money into savings. Others consistently put a little money into savings. Then one day, the occasional people assume the consistent people are lucky that they have so much money set aside. No. It was not luck. It was consistency.

Some people occasionally go on a diet and try to eat healthy. Others consistently eat healthy as their diet. Then one day, the occasional people think the consistent people are lucky because they're in such good shape and don't struggle with their weight. No. It was not luck. It was consistency.

You might meet people who live amazing lives for God. It's easy to conclude, "Man, that would be so cool. They're so lucky God chose to use them like that!"

Once again, not luck. Consistency.

Remember what we saw with Daniel? God granted him favor and used him in all kinds of extraordinary ways. Lucky? No! We were given a key insight into his life: Daniel prayed to God three times every day. We read that and think, *Well, I pray too. I mean, not always. And not three times a day. And, well, maybe not every day.* I wonder: What could God do with your life if you prayed to him three times every day? We pray occasionally. Daniel prayed consistently.

Successful people do consistently what other people do occasionally.

For his 2008 book, *Outliers: The Story of Success*, Malcolm Gladwell studied successful people. What common thread did he find to explain their success? The answer: ten thousand hours. He discovered that, across the board, people who became great at something put in ten thousand hours of practice.[38]

It's not luck. It's consistency.

Do you remember when wide receiver Odell Beckham Jr. made an unbelievable one-handed catch that many consider the greatest ever?[39] People saw the catch and probably thought, *Obviously, that takes natural skill, but there was some serious luck happening there too!* Then the reports came out that Beckham has practiced making one-handed catches—every single day—since he was in high school. *Ohhhh.* It wasn't luck. It was practice. Consistent practice. Ten thousand hours.

Gladwell says the common denominator with all the successful people he studied was that they fell in love with practice. Or we could say they fell in love with training. The greats don't try, they train. They commit to practicing every day.[40]

Performance coach Alan Stein Jr. spent fifteen years working with some of the best athletes in the world. One day, Stein asked

Kobe Bryant if he could watch the athlete's workout routine. Bryant agreed, telling Stein to meet him at the gym the next day—at four in the morning. Stein arrived a little early, only to find Bryant already in a full sweat. He was doing a very basic, boring workout. When Stein asked Bryant why, the basketball legend answered, "Why do you think I'm the best player in the world? Because I never, ever get bored with the basics."[41]

In an article on his insane work ethic, Bryant explained what propelled him to all-world status: "It's a constant quest to try to be better today than you were yesterday."[42] Yep. Remember, training is doing today what you can do today so you can do tomorrow what you can't do today.

People who are successful in sports win by practicing. The next time you see a sports report on your favorite team showing footage of practice, notice how every player, even the highest-paid athlete on the team, does basic drills. They get there day by day, a little at a time.

People who are successful in their careers or marriages got there a little at a time. People who are in great shape physically or financially got there a little at a time. People who are amazing at parenting or repairing cars or open-heart surgery or crossword puzzles or writing code or Frisbee golf or writing books or acting or taking companies public or preaching sermons or editing videos or performing stand-up comedy or break dancing or juggling chainsaws got there a little at a time.

Today, through small and consistent decisions, you're getting somewhere a little at a time.

Where are you going?

Where will you be in ten years? Who will you be?

Exercise 19

Complete the following sentences.

One thing I have done occasionally that I want to become fanatically consistent at doing is:

I can begin (or increase my efforts) to put in my ten thousand hours by:

Principle 19

Successful people do consistently what other people do occasionally.

Wealth from get-rich-quick schemes quickly disappears; wealth from hard work grows over time.

—Proverbs 13:11 NLT

4.2 You in Ten

What if you had met Elon Musk in 1995 when he left Stanford University to start his first software company? Would you have thought, *Wow! There's just something different about this kid. I think he's going to be the richest person in the world one day.* Or might you have just thought he was a quirky, eccentric college dropout?

What if you'd met Simone Biles when she was fourteen years old and competing in her first classic gymnastics event in her hometown of Houston, Texas? Would you have been able to single her out and say, "In ten years this girl is going to be the world record holder for earning the most gold medals?" Or might you have paid her no attention in the lineup of girls, all very similar in age, size, and skill?

What if I told you I could predict what your life will be like in ten years? What if I could tell whether you'll be:

- Better off financially
- Closer to God
- Healthier
- More together than ever
- Happier
- In a circle of good friends

Chances are, I could. I don't have some special ability or a Magic 8 Ball. (Well, I do have a Magic 8 Ball, but every time I shake it, I get, "Ask Again Later.") But I could make an accurate prediction.

> **The life you are living right now is shaping the life you will live tomorrow.**

How?

Because your habits today are telegraphing your future. The life you are living right now is shaping the life you will live tomorrow.

We all have the best intentions, but intentions don't determine direction. Actions do.

We all have hopes. But hoping for a different future doesn't lead to a different future. Hope doesn't change your life. Habits do.

So if you keep doing what you've been doing, you'll keep getting what you've been getting. The life you're living today is shaping the life you'll live tomorrow.

The life you want can be the life you're living in ten years. But you will not get there because of your intentions, your hopes, or a few "lucky breaks."

But like Kobe Bryant, Elon Musk, Simone Biles, and all the other ten-thousand-hour people, you can get there. And when you do, it will be the result of countless seemingly small decisions, done consistently over time.

Let's focus on two essential components you'll need to become the you that you want to be.

The first component is "small." Remember: the small things no one sees can lead to the big results everyone wants. The issue with small things is that they are easy to do but also easy not to do. They never seem significant. Ignoring or skipping them always feels acceptable. But you sculpt your life with the small stuff.

The second component is "consistent." Doing the small thing once is insignificant. Doing the right small things over and over has magnitude you cannot measure.

To drive home the importance of both of these dynamics, imagine you are on a full flight, and the attendant has closed the aircraft door. As the pilot is backing away from the gate, he makes the following announcement: "Ladies and gentlemen, we have been told a small part has fallen off one of the engines, but to get you to your destination on time, we're going to ignore it and take off. Oh, and also we normally do routine, consistent maintenance before every flight, but again, to be on time today, we're going to forego that and get you in the air. Now, sit back, relax, and enjoy your flight." How would you feel about small and consistent then?

For now, I hope we can agree: getting the life you want will be the result of countless seemingly small decisions, done consistently over time.

Let's go to God's Word to learn why.

You build your life one brick at a time.

That's what Nehemiah might have said.

His story in the Bible provides a great illustration of what this looks like.

Nehemiah was the cupbearer for Artaxerxes, the King of Persia. The Persians had overthrown the Babylonians. Remember how we learned in Daniel's story that the Babylonians invaded Jerusalem? That happened seventy years before Nehemiah's time. The Babylonians had destroyed the city and taken most of the people. But some Jews still remained in the wreckage of Jerusalem.

When you hear about the state of Jerusalem it may remind you of some aspect of your life. Because of some tragic or devastating event, you might feel like a part of your life is in ruins.

Though he had lived his entire life in Persia, Nehemiah was Jewish. When he got word of how bad things were in his homeland, he "sat down and wept" (Neh. 1:4).

You might feel like crying over how some area of your life is not what it was or what it should be.

Nehemiah could have thought, *There's nothing I can do. It has been that way a long time. I have no power to effect change.* (Sound familiar?)

But he didn't. He took action. Nehemiah believed he could make a difference, so he took responsibility. Here's how he described the first step in his plan: "For some days I mourned and fasted and prayed before the God of heaven" (Neh. 1:4). Nehemiah began with prayer, which is the right place to start. When you don't know what to do, go to the one who does.

Nehemiah then took some strategic steps to get permission to go rebuild the wall that was supposed to encircle and protect Jerusalem. He didn't rely on good intentions or hope. He created a game plan.

We also need to develop a strategy if we are going to rebuild a critical piece of our lives.

Nehemiah arrived in Jerusalem and let the people know of his plan to rebuild the wall. They thought he was cuckoo for Cocoa Puffs.[43] The wall had been in crumbles for 140 years. No one ever had the gall to consider rebuilding because, in their minds, the work simply could not be done.

That may be how you feel about the change you want. You think there's just no way.

But Nehemiah convinced the people they had to do something; the wall was necessary to protect them from invading armies.

Nehemiah issued work assignments and, under his leadership, the people hesitantly started to rebuild the wall. Do you know how they did it? If you don't have an advanced degree in wall construction, this may be too intricate for you to understand, but they built the wall—are you ready? For sure? Okay. They built the wall one brick at a time.

Sorry, you actually don't need a PhD in wallology. That's super easy for anyone to understand. Nehemiah and the cautious citizens of Jerusalem built the wall brick by brick, one at a time. That's the only way to build a wall. (Pink Floyd also taught us this concept in 1979.)

The same is true for us. We will change our lives one small habit at a time. I'll say it again: getting the life you want will be the result of countless seemingly small decisions, done consistently over time.

The Israelites started building the wall, and it was actually happening! Progress was slow, but there was progress. Soon, they were building not only the wall but optimism in the ranks. *This might be possible after all? Maybe we can do this? Maybe Nehemiah isn't crazy?*

Optimism sprouted, but it wasn't long before they faced opposition and obstacles. Some of the most significant resistance came from the voices of two people, Sanballat and Tobiah. These guys were haters who ridiculed the idea that the Jews could accomplish their goal. (These guys would have been huge on Facebook.) Sanballat taunted, "What are those feeble Jews doing? Will they restore their wall? Will they offer sacrifices? Will they finish in a day? Can they bring the stones back to life from those heaps of rubble—burned as they are?" (Neh. 4:2).

Wow. That sounds *so* familiar. Because every time I try to change my life or accomplish a goal, I hear whispers in my head too. Those whispers ask mockingly:

- *What are you doing?*
- *Will you really restore this part of your life?*
- *Do you think you can accomplish this in a day?*
- *That part of your life is dead.*
- *You think you can bring it back to life?*

Sometimes the antagonism comes not from within. We may also have some Sanballats in our lives who openly doubt our ability to change.

Despite the critics, the people continued to build the wall—one brick at a time. Nehemiah gave this progress report: "So we rebuilt the wall till all of it reached half its height, for the people worked with all their heart" (Neh. 4:6).

You might think reaching that halfway point would be something to celebrate. Nope. Because halfway is a challenging place. You can see you've made progress. *Yeaaah!* But you can also see how far you have to go. *Craaap!* That's exactly why halfway through is such an easy place to get discouraged.

That's what happened with the Jews. "Meanwhile, the people in Judah said, 'The strength of the laborers is giving out'" (Neh. 4:10). They thought they would be farther along. They became disappointed. They considered quitting.

You are likely to find yourself at that same place. It usually happens like this:

1. You begin by defining a win.
2. You make some progress and feel good about it.
3. You realize you still have a long way to go.

After defining your destination and making some headway, you discover the journey is slower and longer than you expected. Feeling disillusioned, you wonder, *Why am I not farther along by now?* Quitting sounds kind of nice.

That's the obstacle we all have to conquer. You build your life one brick at a time. So consistency is the key. Consistency over the long haul. You'll want to quit, but you can't because what you're pursuing is way too important.

So what do you do when you want to quit?

In his story, we see that whenever Nehemiah felt discouraged, he prayed. *Twelve times* we see him face opposition and, in response, pray. Nehemiah knew a truth we need to understand: we cannot consistently continue to do the right things, over the long haul, in our own power.

We need power we don't possess. We need God's power. We need to access God's power. That's why we're going to learn how to do just that in the last section of this book.

Nehemiah kept praying and encouraging the people. They kept working. And they were making progress. The circumstances were never perfect, but nothing ever is.

Here's another huge truth for us to learn: we must value progress over perfection. Let me repeat—we must value progress over perfection.

You will trip. You will fall. Your journey won't be perfect. But keep moving in the right direction. Your goal is not perfection, it's progress.

Nehemiah and his team kept working, and finally, they accomplished the goal. The wall was built!

Care to guess how long it took them?

Your goal is not perfection, it's progress.

"So on October 2 the wall was finished—just fifty-two days after we had begun" (Neh. 6:15 NLT).

Wait! *Fifty-two days?*

For 140 *years* the people lived in danger without a wall. For 140 years they thought there was nothing they could do about their problem. And the change they needed took place in only *fifty-two days*?! All that time when they didn't have what they wanted, they could have accomplished it in less than two months?

That's crazy to me! But also very cool.

Change took fifty-two days. I believe *you* will see significant change in your life if you consistently (remember, not perfectly, consistently) do your strategic habit.

I'm sure you have already decided, but one last time I want to ask you: What is the strategic habit you need to start?

- Spending ten minutes a day in prayer?
- Limiting your time on Instagram to thirty minutes or less a day?
- Walking a mile after dinner each night?
- Writing three things you're thankful for in a gratitude journal at the end of every day?
- Taking the first ten minutes of each day to prioritize and plan your time?
- Planning a weekly date with your spouse or kid?
- Tithing, to help you grow your trust in God?

All of these are easy to do. But they're also easy not to do. That's the problem. You can feel like it's no big deal to skip them. But not anymore, right? You're going to commit to consistently doing your strategic habit. With God's help, you'll be building your life—one brick at a time. If you start consistently doing that habit, what positive impact might it have on your life, even in just fifty-two days?

For years psychologists told us that a habit could be formed in just twenty-one days. Recent studies have refuted that finding, reporting that, for the average person, it takes sixty-six days to create a lasting habit.[44] The good news for those of us who may have been discouraged by an unsuccessful twenty-one days is that if the Jews could build their wall under opposition and threats in fifty-two days, we can make a significant change if we stay consistent for sixty-six days—two months and some change.

Also what's the habit you need to strategically stop doing?

- Using a credit card?
- Raising your voice in anger?
- Hanging out with friends who have a negative influence on you?

- Watching a certain TV show?
- Spending money on things (cable TV, Netflix, Starbucks, eating out for lunch, etc.) that keep you from paying off debt?

What do you need to stop doing? I wonder, if you stopped doing it for just fifty-two days, what positive impact might it have on your life?

I know this: Each day, the effect will seem inconsequential. You may not see any difference at first. But change *is* happening. You *are* changing your life.

You're doing it one brick at a time. That's what Nehemiah would say. Brick by brick.

God uses another metaphor for how it happens. You build your life one seed at a time. Seed by seed.

Exercise 20

What area of your life is not what it was or what it should be?

Begin with prayer. Ask God to help you develop a strategy:

List a few bricks you can focus on in the next few days to take small and consistent steps.

Principle 20

We need a power we don't possess.

Value progress over perfection.

"LORD, the God of heaven, the great and awesome God, who keeps his covenant of love with those who love him and keep his commandments, let your ear be attentive and your eyes open to hear the prayer your servant is praying before you day and night."

—Nehemiah 1:5–6

4.3 You Reap What You Sow

I've been saying that habits shape your life. Perhaps you've been wondering, *Where does God tell us that in the Bible?*

Galatians 6.

But God doesn't use the word *habits*. He uses the metaphor of seeds. Why? In biblical times, people lived in an agricultural society. Nothing was manufactured or cranked out in fast-food joints. Food had to be grown one ingredient at a time. Their lives and economy were based largely on farming.

People back then would understand the concept of planting seeds and harvesting crops, so here's what God inspired Paul to write: "Do not be deceived: God cannot be mocked. A man reaps what he sows. Whoever sows to please their flesh, from the flesh will reap destruction; whoever sows to please the Spirit, from the Spirit will reap eternal life. Let us not become weary in doing good, for at the proper time we will reap a harvest if we do not give up" (Gal. 6:7–9).

For us non-agrarians, let's establish some definitions.

- To sow means to plant—to put seed in the ground.
- To reap means to gather the fruit—the result of the seed planted.

So the passage starts, "Do not be deceived." The idea is: don't be led astray. Don't be fooled, or stupid.

It continues, "God cannot be mocked." The Greek word translated "mocked" means to snub or thumb your nose at someone. You can do that to someone—but not God. Don't be deceived, God can't be mocked. You might fool a lot of people, but you're not going to fool God.

The next words are, "A man reaps what he sows." *That's* what we need to understand and not be stupid about. What does that mean?

- You will harvest what you plant.
- You will get out what you put in.
- Your outcomes will be determined by your inputs.
- The results of your life will be based on the decisions you make, the habits you stake, and the habits you break.

Paul gives us a spiritual example about sowing to the flesh or the Spirit. The flesh refers to our sinful nature. Some sow (or plant seeds) to the flesh, meaning they do what's wrong, ungodly, and sinful. The result? They reap (or harvest) destruction. Bad decisions lead to bad consequences.

Others sow (or plant seeds) to the Spirit, meaning they allow themselves to be led and empowered by the Holy Spirit, so they do what honors God. The result? They reap (or harvest) eternal life. So if you live your life with and for God, that's what you're going to get out of it. Not just now but (especially) eternally. If you live your life for yourself, ignoring God, apart from him, that's what you're going to get out of it. Not just now but (especially) eternally.

But it's not just true spiritually and eternally. This is the way all of life works. We reap what we sow.

There's a law at work. Not a law like "You must do this!" More like how gravity is a law of nature. It's how the world works. You don't have to like it. You don't have to agree with it. Gravity will work for you, and on you, the same way it works with everyone. If you jump, you will go up. Then gravity will bring you down. We say people get "tripped up," but that's not true. People always trip down. Gravity is a natural law.

God tells us there is a law of sowing and reaping.

If you plant apple seeds, you get apple trees. If you plant orange seeds, don't be deceived; don't be stupid and expect apples. You can picture a farmer out in his fields: *Wait. What's this? I wanted apples. Why did I get oranges?* It's because you planted orange seeds! If you plant corn, you're going to reap corn. Don't plant corn if you want pineapples. That would be stupid. When you put a certain type of seed in the ground, you get a harvest that corresponds with the seed you planted.

Every. Single. Time. You reap what you sow.

True in agriculture. True in life.

If you plant good habits, you'll get good outcomes. If you plant bad habits, don't be deceived and expect good outcomes.

Wait. What's this? I didn't want this. Why is this happening?

If you plant good habits, you'll get good outcomes. If you plant bad habits, don't be deceived and expect good outcomes.

Because that's what you planted. You fooled yourself into thinking you could plant one thing and reap another.

Sounds crazy that someone might do that, but it happens all the time. A guy sows seeds of lust. He checks out girls at the gym, girls at his office, girls online. But he expects to have a good marriage. Then, when his marriage struggles, he's confused. *Wait. What's this?* It's what you planted.

A woman sows seeds of criticism and negativity but expects good friends. People avoid her. She's lonely. She thinks, *Wait. What's this? I guess I have bad friends.* No. It's what you planted.

A recent college graduate sows seeds of showing up late for

work and giving a halfhearted effort but expects a promotion. When someone else is given the promotion, the young adult thinks, *Wait. What's this? Man, my boss isn't fair!* No. It's what you planted.

Some dude eats anything he wants. *Praise the Lord and pass the Doritos!* He doesn't exercise. He drinks a six-pack on Friday to celebrate that it's Friday. And a six-pack on Saturday cause, hey, it's Saturday. And a six pack on Sunday because it's the last day of the weekend. He ends up thirty-five pounds overweight in his forties and with cirrhosis in his fifties. *Hey! What's this? This isn't fair! Is God punishing me for something I did when I was a kid?* No. It's not a punishment. It's a harvest. You are reaping what you've sown.

When people mess up their marriages, friendships, or careers, they get upset and often blame God. *Ummm, no.* God didn't do this to you. *You* did this to you.

If you plant good habits, you'll get good outcomes.

If you plant bad habits, don't expect good outcomes.

You reap what you sow.

If you don't like what you're reaping, change what you're sowing. If you don't like the harvest, change the seed.

Here's a divine assignment: Take an honest, prayerful look at the disappointing parts of your life. Ask God to help you search your heart. Then pinpoint the habits that have led to each aspect of your life that isn't what you want. Avoid having a victim mentality or blaming others. That will not help. Take responsibility by identifying the habits you've sown that have led to your harvest. Then decide on a type of seed you will consistently plant to get a better harvest.

If you don't like what you're reaping, change what you're sowing.

Because you reap what you sow.

And it's actually even bigger than that.

Exercise 21

Here's the assignment we just covered. Use this pattern for as many areas of life as you need to address.

God, I have sown _____ *and*
have reaped _____ *because of*
my habit of _____.

To change this outcome, I need to start or stop my habit of _____
_____, *so help me to plant the seeds of*
_____ *so I can reap* _____
_____.

Principle 21

If you don't like what you're reaping, change what you're sowing. If you don't like the harvest, change the seed.

You will always harvest what you plant. Those who live only to satisfy their own sinful nature will harvest decay and death from that sinful nature. But those who live to please the Spirit will harvest everlasting life from the Spirit.

—Galatians 6:7–8 NLT

4.4 You Reap More Than You Sow

So now that you've wrapped your brain around the idea that you reap what you sow, it's time to blow your mind.

You don't just reap *what* you sow.

You reap *more* than you sow.

That's the way agriculture works. If you put a kernel of wheat in the ground, it will produce a stalk with three heads of wheat. A head can contain fifteen to thirty-five kernels. So one kernel produces about one hundred kernels. If you plant those kernels, they'll produce about ten thousand kernels.

True in agriculture. Also true in life. You reap more than you sow. You won't just get out what you put in. You will get out way more than you put in.

But why do you reap more than you sow?

There are two powerful factors at play, but we often ignore them.

The Cumulative Effect

The cumulative effect is the powerful outcome produced by an action that happens, even if it's small, over and over across a long period of time.

Let's say I make you an offer. I will give you a magic penny that doubles every day for one month. So on the first day it's one penny. The second day it's two. The third day it's four, and so on.

But then I give you an option: I'll give you that penny or $5 million.

Which should you choose? The $5 million, right? Wrong! (Thanks for playing. Don, tell our guest about the lovely parting gifts.)

At the end of the thirty days, that penny would be worth $5,368,709. Unless it's a thirty-one-day month, then double the extra day and it would be worth $10,737,418. You'd be a fool to take the $5 million.[45]

But so often we settle because we discount the cumulative effect: the powerful impact of something happening over and over for a long period of time.

The Compound Effect

The second powerful factor we need to understand is the compound effect. This is typically called "compounding interest," used in reference to finances. This is the interest you get on the interest. Say you put $1,000 into an index fund. Then you get 10 percent interest. At the end of the year, you'd have $1,100. If you leave the interest alone, the next year you will earn interest not only on the original $1,000 investment but also on the $100 interest you gained. At the same 10 percent interest rate, a year later your account will have $1,210. Each year you will earn interest on your initial investment *and* on the accumulating interest.

If you let the $1,000 sit in that account for twenty-five years, it will become more than $10,000. Albert Einstein was supposed to have said, "The most powerful force in the universe is compound interest."[46]

Grasping the significance of these principles will change your life. In fact, they have already shaped your life.

Who you are today is because of the cumulative and compound effects. Who you become tomorrow will be because of the cumulative and compound effects. In his special message at the beginning of Darren Hardy's book *The Compound Effect*, Anthony Robbins writes, "Decisions shape your destiny.... Little, everyday decisions will either take you to the life you desire or to disaster by default."[47]

That is so true! So let's make those principles work for us, not against us.

> Who you are today is because of cumulative and compound effects.

Let me give you some examples so you can better see how these principles play out in our lives.

Financial

If a forty-year-old wants to have $1 million in savings by age sixty-five and gets a typical interest rate for a good index or mutual fund:

- They have to invest $20 a day, every day.
- That's $7,300 invested every year.
- That's about $182,500 invested to have $1 million at age sixty-five.

If a twenty-year-old wants to have $1 million in savings at age sixty-five:

- They have to invest only $2 a day.
- That's barely more than $700 a year.
- That's about $30,000 invested to have $1 million at age sixty-five.

Wow!
Read those numbers again.
Why?

Because the cumulative effect of compounding interest is crazy.

If you want to win financially, start now and consistently do the small, right thing.

Physical

Have you ever had a hundred-calorie pack? The problem you discover when you open a hundred-calorie pack is that there's virtually nothing in there! Get a hundred-calorie bag of OREO Thins. You will learn they're not really OREO cookies, they are *very* thin, and there are very few of them in the bag. *What did you expect for a hundred calories? Actual cookies?*

One hundred calories is almost nothing.

When you choose to eat it, the extra hundred-calorie snack will feel like a nothing decision.

But check this out: you burn a certain number of calories every day. If you eat just one hundred fewer calories (the equivalent of one of those little skimpy bags) than you burn every day, you will lose ten pounds in a year.

If you eat just one hundred more calories than you burn every day, you will gain ten pounds in a year.

That's a twenty-pound difference.

One hundred calories is like nothing, but one hundred calories daily is something. Because you are adding the magic ingredients of repetition and time. James Clear writes, "Time magnifies the margin between success and failure. It will multiply whatever you feed it. Good habits make time your ally. Bad habits make time your enemy."[48]

A small difference each day adds up and multiplies over time.

A small difference each day adds up and multiplies over time.

It's the cumulative effect of compounding interest. Or calories.

Spiritual

This is harder to see because it's not quantifiable, but these principles also apply spiritually.

You read about a spiritual hero—like a Billy Graham. Or you meet someone who is close to God and has a powerful impact on people for him. You think, *I want that. I wish I were like that person.*

Well, you can be.

There's a reason those people are tight with God and have become a spiritual force. They consistently do spiritual disciplines that connect them to God. Ask. My guess is they'll tell you they read their Bibles and pray just about every day and attend church and a small group every week. John Wesley got up every morning at four o'clock to pray! Martin Luther prayed for three hours every day.[49]

Listening to one sermon or praying one day or doing one Bible study will make only a small difference. But with consistency, those small differences make a big difference. They compound.

C. S. Lewis, a brilliant Christian thinker and author, wrote about this in his book *Mere Christianity*: "Good and evil both increase at compound interest. That is why the little decisions you and I make every day are of such infinite importance. The smallest good act today is the capture of a strategic point from which, a few months later, you may be able to go on to victories you never dreamed of. An apparently trivial indulgence in lust or anger today is the loss of a ridge or railway line or bridgehead from which the enemy may launch an attack otherwise impossible."[50]

Making a wise decision or doing something good for God today may feel insignificant. But keep doing it. You have no idea the significance it could grow to have in the future.

The inverse is also true.

When we don't engage in an essential spiritual habit, or when we choose to sin, even if we think of it as an isolated incident, it's not. The Bible says that one little choice can "give the devil a foothold" (Eph. 4:27) to enter and work in our lives. We're told that one little disobedience, one little sin, can "harden [our] hearts" and has a way of "turning [us] away from the living God" (Heb. 3:8, 12 NLT).

When we submit to and obey God, it may seem like a onetime decision. It's not. We are training ourselves to be faithful. That one act of obedience proves us trustworthy, trains us in faithfulness, and softens our hearts to continue to say yes to God (Ezek. 11:19–20; 36:26–27).

It's the cumulative effect of compounding interest.

The Small Stuff

There was a book some years ago that encouraged people not to "sweat the small stuff" and to realize "it's all small stuff."[51]

That may be true when it comes to worrying, but there is no such thing as "small stuff" when it comes to our habits and decisions.

Because of the cumulative effect and compounding interest:

- Saving two dollars a day and putting it into a retirement account is not small stuff.
- Eating an extra hundred-calorie bag is not small stuff.
- Deciding to skip working out today is not small stuff.
- Telling your spouse "I love you" *again* is not small stuff.
- Having one more drink is not small stuff.
- Writing an encouraging letter to your child is not small stuff.
- Taking a couple of minutes to pray before you start your day is not small stuff.

That's how life works. What you do every day is turning you into the person you will become and leading you into the life you will live. What you do occasionally does not make a difference. What you do consistently makes *all* the difference. Because of the cumulative effect and compounding interest, a small change can change everything.

It's the law of reaping and sowing.

You reap what you sow.

And you reap more than you sow.

But wait, there's even more.

Exercise 22

Give some examples from your life of when you have seen the effect of cumulative and compound choices at work—positive or negative.

Financial:

Physical:

Spiritual:

What was the smallest decision you ever made that had the greatest impact on your life?

What was the greatest "small stuff" act that impacted your life, such as a word of encouragement, an act of kindness, or a simple gift?

What was the last "small stuff" act of your own that impacted someone else?

Principle 22

You reap more than you sow.

A small change can change everything.

To those who use well what they are given, even more will be given, and they will have an abundance.

—Matthew 25:29 NLT

4.5 You Reap after You Sow

The farmer wants avocados. He knows the law of sowing and reaping, so he plants avocado seeds.

Picture him taking those *big* seeds and putting them in the ground. And then him staring at the ground.

Well?

A minute passes.

Well??

He continues to impatiently stare at the ground where he planted those *humongous* seeds. Another minute goes by.

Well?! What's going on here?

A farmer would never do that. Farmers know that you not only reap what you sow but also reap *after* you sow. The harvest comes in a different season. You plant in one season and then have to wait until another season for the harvest.

The same is true in life. But we so often miss this. That's why we get discouraged. That's why we wrongly conclude that small decisions don't matter. It's why we're tempted to quit.

- "We want our marriage to be better. We've been going to counseling for a month. We're still arguing. We quit!"
- "I decided I wanted to lose weight. I went to the gym the last two weeks. Three times each week. And I lost only one pound! I quit."

- "I read the Bible every day this week, but I don't feel any closer to God. I quit."
- "I have $22,000 in student loans. I decided to pay them off quicker by bringing lunch to work instead of buying it. I did it all month. I saved only three hundred bucks. That's not going to pay off my debt. I quit!"

No, don't quit! Keep going to counseling. Keep going to the gym. Keep reading your Bible. And "only" three hundred bucks saved each month will add up to almost $4,000 by the end of the year. If you keep going, you'll soon pay off the whole $22,000. (Also remember, paying off debt decreases both accrued interest and the principal owed.)

Don't quit! Remember, getting the life you want will be the result of countless seemingly small decisions, done consistently over time. They will feel insignificant, but with every action, you are choosing a direction.

Let's revisit the passage in Galatians 6. Verse 9 always inspires me: "Let us not become weary in doing good, for at the proper time we will reap a harvest if we do not give up."

It's so easy to "become weary in doing good." Trust me, I'm a pastor.

When your marriage or health or finances or spiritual impact are struggling, you think, *It's bad, and it will never be better.* You grow weary of trying to make things better. You tried to change, but it didn't work. And that confirmed your belief that you are pathetic and will always be stuck.

Those. Are. Lies.

That's why we're encouraged not to become weary or give up. You're in one season, and if you don't quit, one day you are going to wake up in a new season. And you will reap a harvest. You'll realize your hard work, your discipline, your sacrifices, and your faithfulness were never wasted. Your efforts were just being stored up.

Imagine putting a pot full of room-temperature water on a stove. If the fire burns consistently, the water will heat up to 85 degrees. Then 97 degrees. Then 114 degrees. Then 139. Then 187. Then 201. Eventually, it will get to 211 degrees. What will you have then? Really hot water. But then, finally, the water will go up another degree. Then what will you have? Boiling water.

> Your hard work, your discipline, your sacrifices, and your faithfulness are never wasted. Your efforts are just being stored up.

If you're waiting for water to boil, at 211 degrees, you'll be frustrated. *I've been waiting forever! The fire doesn't seem to be doing its job.* In fact, you will have been waiting the longest and feel the most frustrated at 211 degrees. But the water has never been closer to boiling. And the fire has been having its effect. It's just that the effect has been storing up. If you wait another minute, you will have 212-degree water that's boiling.

The same is true in our lives.

What if you give up and stop praying for your prodigal child at 211 degrees and the next day would have been the boiling point—the breakthrough?

What if you give up and stop speaking encouragement to your spouse at 211 degrees and the next word would have been the boiling point—the reconciliation?

What if you give up and quit calling to check on your non-believing friend at 211 degrees and the next call would have been the boiling point—the surrender?

James Clear calls the waiting between sowing and reaping the "Plateau of Latent Potential" or the "Valley of Disappointment."[52] That's when we are tempted to quit. And that's why we need to understand that we reap *after* we sow.

In the Valley of Disappointment, we feel like all of our trying has been worthless. No. "This work was not wasted," Clear writes, "It was simply being stored."[53]

One day, you wake up and realize your marriage is better than you ever thought it could be.

One day, you wake up and realize you can fit in your "skinny" clothes again.

One day, you wake up and find yourself leading a Bible study when you used to feel like you'd never be worthy to do something like that.

One day, you wake up debt free and realize you're giving more generously than you ever imagined.

And people will look at your life and say, "You're so lucky."

Ha!

Luck did not happen. What happened was you started doing consistently what you used to do occasionally. And consistency made all the difference. One brick at a time.

They'll think it's luck because the small things no one has seen—the seeds in the ground—have led to the big results everyone now wants.

They didn't see you getting up early. Working out. Praying. Fasting. Going to your support group. Saying no when you wanted to say yes. Training. Confessing. Sweating. Holding your tongue. Writing encouraging notes. Putting your phone down. Getting counseling.

They won't know about the grind, the perseverance, the pain. How you fell down but got back up. The desperate prayers. Your daily discipline. How you wanted to quit but refused to give up.

> **You will reap a harvest if you don't give up.**

They won't know about any of that. They'll just envy the changes you've made and think you're "lucky" or #blessed.

But only if you don't quit. You will reap a harvest if you don't give up.

So don't give up:

- Believing
- Praying
- Sharing your faith
- Fighting to stay pure
- Getting up early
- Saying "I love you"
- Asking
- Walking forward
- Having faith that God will free you from addiction
- Studying
- Forgiving
- Climbing out of debt
- Sacrificing
- Choosing what you want most over what you want now

Keep doing it.

Consistently.

Day after day.

One right decision at a time.

Don't judge the success of each day by what you reap. Judge success by the seeds you sow.

Did you do the right things?

Did you honor God?

Did you take a step in the right direction?

You don't become successful when you achieve the goal in the future. You are successful when you do your strategic habit today. Success is doing it consistently instead of occasionally.

You won't see the results you want today. Be patient. You've planted the right seeds. The harvest will come.

It won't be because you had the best intentions or high hopes but because your actions determined your direction. Your habits changed you. Day after day, you shaped your life by doing the right small things. They added up and multiplied, accumulated and compounded, and turned you into the person you're going to be in ten years. I can predict it. I can see Future You and:

You. Are. Awesome.

You will reap a harvest.

If you don't give up.

■ ■ ■

I hope and pray I've inspired you.

I hope you're fired up.

But I've got some bad news.

I don't want to say it. Especially now, when you feel ready to take on the world. But I have to tell you the truth.

So here goes: you're not capable of this.

You cannot consistently continue to do the right things, over the long haul, in your own power. Remember that?

Let's be honest.

You will get discouraged, and you will quit. I mean, you know yourself. You don't possess what you need for success.

Unless you get the secret sauce.

Exercise 23

Where have you given up and need God's help to get started again?

Where are you struggling and being tempted to give up and need God's help to endure?

Where are you experiencing a harvest and reaping more than you have sown?

Principle 23

You will reap a harvest if you don't give up.

They are like trees planted along the riverbank,
    bearing fruit each season.
Their leaves never wither,
    and they prosper in all they do.

—Psalm 1:3 NLT

Part 5

God's Power. Not Willpower.

5.1 I Can't

She sat on a toilet for two years.

A thirty-five-year-old woman in Ness City, Kansas, sat on a toilet and did not get up until her boyfriend finally called the police two years later. The Ness County sheriff explained that, over the two years, her skin had grown around the seat. She had become stuck to the toilet. Apparently, her boyfriend brought her food and water, and asked her to come out of the bathroom, every day.

Her reply? "Maybe tomorrow."[54]

When I first heard that story, I didn't know what to think. I had so many questions. Mostly, *Why didn't she just get up?*

Then I realized—I have been that woman. I've had times when I felt stuck. Looking back now, I can't believe I stayed in the same situation for so long. I remember feeling helpless. I wanted to get unstuck but felt powerless. Just like her, I'd think, *Maybe tomorrow*.

There's likely an area of your life where you feel stuck right now:

- You and your spouse have been stuck in the same unhealthy relational patterns for years.
- You and your teenager have been stuck in the same unhealthy relational patterns for years.
- You're stuck looking at your phone and realize you have some kind of social media addiction.
- You're stuck in a job you hate.

- You're stuck with a critical, complaining spirit you know turns others off.
- You're stuck with high cholesterol or blood pressure.
- You're stuck spiritually, knowing there is so much more for you to experience with God if only you'd take those next steps of faith.

You might admit it's worse than stuck. Your situation feels dead.

You may believe your marriage is dead. The passion has passed. The love is lost. What's left feels lifeless.

Your money situation might seem buried six feet under debt. It feels like there's no way you can dig yourself out. Your finances feel dead.

How do you get unstuck? How do you get undead?

We've looked at some of the apostle Paul's writings, but you may not know his story. Paul was Jewish. When Christianity started, he was violently opposed to the movement. But then he had an incredible encounter with Jesus—after Jesus rose from the dead. Paul actually experienced the risen Christ in a supernatural way.

Overnight, Paul went from being a Christian killer to a Christian pastor. God did miracles through Paul, including raising the dead. He became a remarkable, incredibly devoted follower of Jesus, as well as one of the greatest preachers, church planters, and spiritual giants in the history of the world. Yet, in a letter to the Christians in Rome, he wrote about feeling stuck and trying his best to change. But the change didn't last, so he'd feel stuck again.

> I don't really understand myself, for I want to do what is right, but I don't do it. Instead, I do what I hate. But if I know that what I am doing is wrong, this shows that I agree that the law is good. So I am not the one doing wrong; it is sin living in me that does it.

And I know that nothing good lives in me, that is, in my sinful nature. I want to do what is right, but I can't. I want to do what is good, but I don't. I don't want to do what is wrong, but I do it anyway. But if I do what I don't want to do, I am not really the one doing wrong; it is sin living in me that does it.

I have discovered this principle of life—that when I want to do what is right, I inevitably do what is wrong. I love God's law with all my heart. But there is another power within me that is at war with my mind. This power makes me a slave to the sin that is still within me. Oh, what a miserable person I am! Who will free me from this life that is dominated by sin and death?

—Romans 7:15–24 NLT

What Paul wrote to the Romans back then, he could have written to us today. Because we can all relate to what he was feeling. We've all experienced what he was saying, although we might not say it the way he did. In his book *Restore*, my good friend and editor Vince Antonucci paraphrases what Paul wrote. His "updated" and humorous version is the way we might express it today:

I don't really understand myself, for I want to do what is right, but I don't do it. I tell myself not to yell at my kids, then I hear someone yelling at my kids, and I realize it's me. There's something wrong inside of me that leads me to do what I don't want to do.

I tell myself, "Whatever happens, I will not deviate from my diet. I promise I will not make any exceptions!" Then I find a piece of pizza in my mouth. What a miserable person I am. I am a slave to pizza! As I try to understand this power that makes me a slave to sin, I suddenly have a realization—I am now eating brownies! I am a slave to pizza *and* brownies!

I have discovered this principle of life—that when I want to do right, there's always something wrong for me to look at on the Internet. I don't want to look, but there's something in me that does it anyway.

When I am about to tell my wife that she's just like her mother, I know what I am about to do is wrong. That's why I decide not to tell my wife she's just like her mother. Then I find my mouth opening and words coming out. I hear those words. They sound like... "You are just like your mother." It is sin living in me that does that.

Who will free me from this life dominated by the dumb things *me* keeps doing? One thing *me* knows for sure: it's not gonna be *me*![55]

We can all relate to Paul because he was confessing that he was dying inside.

Paul wanted to do what God wanted. But he was stuck in patterns of sin, wrong thinking, bad habits, and addictive behavior.

He had tried. And tried. And nothing had worked.

Been there?

Why was Paul stuck? Why are we stuck? Why don't we make changes that last? So far, we've learned it can be because:

1. We put do before who.
2. We try instead of train.
3. We hope for change instead of starting (and stopping) the right (and wrong) habits.
4. We do occasionally what we should do consistently.

> **We stay stuck because we rely on willpower instead of God's power.**

But there's another reason. It's big. Here it is: we stay stuck because we rely on willpower instead of God's power.

I think I can. That's a problem. Because I can't.

Paul painfully admitted, "I tried. I tried with everything I had. I thought I could. But I can't."

For years, that was the story I kept repeating too. I wanted to change. I would get motivated. I knew I could! Then I would discover, once again, I can't.

One example: I started partying hard in high school and continued into college. I had relatives who were alcoholics, but I thought I could handle it. I knew I could quit whenever I wanted. Until I couldn't. I would decide to stop drinking and end up drinking again. Reality punched me in the face: *I thought I could, but I can't.* I was stuck. It felt like death.

You've been there with your own issue, right?

You want to change in some way. You try. You make progress, then regress. You end up back in the same place. Or maybe end up farther behind?

Why?

Because willpower doesn't work. We think it does, but it doesn't. We think we can, but we can't.

Willpower is like a muscle. If you work it too hard, it becomes fatigued, and what power is there starts to wane.

Researchers have been proving this dynamic for years. In one early study, a group of people was invited into a room, where they were hit by the aroma of fresh-baked cookies. They saw a table with a plate of warm, delicious cookies and a bowl of radishes. (No one has ever used "warm" or "delicious" to describe radishes.) Half of the group was encouraged to enjoy some cookies. The other half was asked to ignore the cookies and instead eat the radishes. (No one has ever used "enjoy" to describe eating radishes.)

After their snack, the group was given thirty minutes to complete a challenging geometric puzzle. The cookie eaters worked on the puzzle for almost nineteen minutes. But the people who were forced to resist the cookies gave up trying to solve the puzzle after about eight minutes. Using willpower to resist the cookies had sapped their (limited) supply of willpower.[56]

Years of research all point to the same conclusion:

> **Willpower is a limited resource. Willpower wilts.**

Willpower is a limited resource. Willpower wilts.

Willpower doesn't work. Still, we try. Because we're desperate to change. We grit our teeth and give it our all. And it works, at first, for a bit, until our willpower wilts.

You recently committed not to eat sweets. Someone brings donuts to your office. You see the donuts but smile because, while it proves the devil is alive and well, you know you will not eat a donut. You've made that promise to yourself!

The second time you walk by you feel equally strong. The third time you take a glance to see what kind of donuts are in the box. The fourth time you think, *Man, that one with chocolate icing and sprinkles looks good. If I were to eat one, that's the one I'd choose.* The fifth time you decide, *Ya know what? Normally, I'd eat two donuts. What if I just ate half? That wouldn't be bad. To eat half a donut instead of two donuts would show amazing restraint!* So you cut one in half (yes, the one with chocolate icing and sprinkles) and eat it.

A half hour later, you mysteriously find yourself back in the break room. You notice no one ate the other half. You can't let it go to waste, so you eat it. Then you tell yourself that putting a full thirty minutes between halves surely makes it less fattening, right?

What happened? You ran out of willpower. Willpower wilts.

Losing the willpower battle can drag us into a cycle of shame. It goes down like this:

"I feel deficient, bad, incomplete."

Why?

Because "I worry all the time and am controlled by fear" or "I'm not close enough to God" or "I'm so rude to people, and I don't want to be."

So you decide you're going to change. "I'm not worrying anymore!" or "I'm gonna wake up early to spend time with God" or "I'll be nice to people even when I'm in a bad mood!"

A burst of motivation mingled with willpower gives you a little success, but it doesn't last.

Why?

Your willpower is depleted, and you find you're back to your old, disappointing self.

That failure overwhelms you with guilt, which reinforces your negative self-assessment. "I don't just *feel* deficient, bad, incomplete. I really *am* deficient, bad, incomplete."

So what do you do? You try again.

This time you're even more determined. You make a little progress, but again your willpower wanes, and you revert to your old, less desirable behavior.

Another taste of failure leads to more guilt. Eventually, you become more convinced that you are fundamentally flawed. "Something is wrong with me, and it will always be wrong with me." You don't just feel shame. You feel like you're drowning in it. You're caught in a vicious cycle, confessing, "I always screw up. I'm a mess, a loser, a total failure. I'm pathetic. I don't have what it takes. I'm worthless."

You beat up your who and give up.

■ ■ ■

Paul slipped into the shame cycle when he cried out in Romans 7, "Oh, what a miserable person I am!" (v. 24 NLT).

Why do we keep spinning through that shame cycle?

Not because we are incapable of change but because we've tried to change in our own power. That's why we stay stuck—because willpower doesn't work.

With his next words, Paul asked the tortured question, "Who will free me from this life that is dominated by sin and death?" (v. 24 NLT).

I get that. You probably get that. That's why you're reading this book.

So what do we do?

Exercise 24

As you work through this exercise, consider this progression:

- After feeling stuck long enough, we can feel dead.
- After we feel dead long enough, we can feel shame.
- After we feel shame, we give in and give up.

Be honest about the depth of any places where you feel you can't change.

Places in my life where I feel stuck:

Places in my life where I feel dead:

Places in my life where I feel shame:

Principle 24

You think you can, but you can't.

I have discovered this principle of life—that
when I want to do what is right, I inevitably do
what is wrong. I love God's law with all my heart.
But there is another power within me that is at war
with my mind. This power makes me a slave to the
sin that is still within me.

—**Romans 7:21–23 NLT**

5.2 But God Can

I've never mentioned the accident before.

In other books, I've shared about my first car. It had multiple personalities, a Dr. Jekyll/Mr. Hyde quality.

Cool: It had a spoiler on the back and eagle stickers on each side!

Not cool: It was a mud-brown Buick.

Cool: I installed an Alpine stereo system!

Not cool: The stereo worked only at night.

I didn't know why at the time. But it was because I mistakenly wired my stereo to my headlights. So if the headlights weren't on, no Van Halen "Jump," no Quiet Riot "Bang Your Head," no Whitesnake "Here I Go Again," no Scorpions "Rock You Like a Hurricane." Definitely not cool.

The car wasn't as cool as I wanted it to be. But then—the accident. This is the part of my car story I've never shared before. I was driving, headlights on, Twisted Sister's "We're Not Gonna Take It" at full volume. The music was inspiring the eagles (not the band, the decals) on my front quarter panels. They were soaring with a bit more defiant independence. Then some knucklehead rear-ended me.

I instantly thought, *We're not gonna take it anymore!* I almost gave Mr. Knucklehead a knuckle sandwich. Instead, I just shot him my best tough-guy look, and we exchanged insurance information.

I said a sad farewell to my eagles, my only-after-dark stereo, and my spoiler and left my car at a body shop to get repaired. A few days later, the mechanic called to let me know my car was ready.

When I arrived, I inspected my cool/not-so-cool ride to make sure everything was as it should be. That's when I noticed:

My Buick Century was the "Sport Coupe" model. It said so right under the spoiler. Or it had before. The guy who'd fixed it painted "Turbo Coupe" instead of "Sport Coupe." *Whaaa?* My Sport Coupe was now a Turbo Coupe? Yes!! A Turbo Coupe had a turbocharged engine! Way. More. Power. A Turbo Coupe increased my cool factor with the guys by like 70 percent and increased my chances with the ladies by maybe 7 percent.

Despite what it said on the back of my car, my Buick Century did not really have more power.

Because willpower doesn't work, you and I really require more power. We can think we're a Turbo Coupe, but we're still just a Sport Coupe.

Paul knew he needed more power. That's why he asked in Romans 7:24, "Who will free me from this life that is dominated by sin and death?" (NLT). That is the question we all need to answer.

But Paul answered his own question with his next sentence in verse 25: "Thank God! The answer is in Jesus Christ our Lord" (NLT).

Paul understood, *I can't get myself unstuck, so I need a power I don't possess.* The power he found was Jesus. Paul discovered, *I can't. But God can.*

Discovering that same truth transformed my life.

I finally realized I couldn't do what I couldn't do because I was trying in my power. Then I learned how to turn to God and access his power. It worked. He worked! I could do what I couldn't do—by his power. I could stop doing what I couldn't stop doing—by his power.

"Thank God! The answer is in Jesus Christ our Lord."

It was all God. God's power.

The good news is that the same power that helped Paul and helped me is available to you. Actually, this is more accurate: the same power that got Jesus out of a grave, resurrected from death to life, is available to you.

Let's look at something Paul wrote in another of his letters: "As for you, you were dead in your transgressions and sins" (Eph. 2:1).

Wow. The reality is, we don't just feel stuck, we are stuck. Worse than stuck, we are dead.

Have you noticed dead people don't have a lot of power? Ask a dead person to help you carry a

> **The same power that got Jesus out of a grave, resurrected from death to life, is available to you.**

heavy box or arm wrestle. Not gonna happen. Dead people don't have a lot of power. And *we* are dead. Powerless.

That's discouraging. But Paul provided some hope-inducing truth. "I also pray that you will understand the incredible greatness of God's power for us who believe him. This is the same mighty power that raised Christ from the dead" (Eph. 1:19–20 NLT).

The same power God used to raise Jesus from the dead is available to you!

If you feel dead in some area of your life, you don't need to stay dead. Why? Because resurrection power is available to you. If you feel stuck, you don't need to stay stuck. Think about it. If God can get Jesus unstuck from death in a grave, he can certainly get you unstuck.

In the next chapter of Ephesians, Paul wrote, "But God is so rich in mercy, and he loved us so much, that even though we were dead because of our sins, he gave us life when he raised Christ from the dead. (It is only by God's grace that you have been saved!)" (2:4–5 NLT).

There are several Bible passages, like this one, that describe how we've messed things up and gotten stuck. Reading them, you can start to feel depressed, but then this amazing word appears—"but."

You've probably never been thankful for God's "but." But you should. Because when God puts his "but" into your situation, it changes everything.

What was is no longer what is because "but God."

What's behind you is not what's ahead of you because "but God."

Your past doesn't have to be your future because "but God."

We were dead, "but God" gave us life, new life, in Jesus.

Why?

Because God is "rich in mercy" and "loved us so much."

Paul then described God's grace. Grace means to get the opposite of what you deserve. God loves us in spite of us, not because of us. He loves us not because of what we do but because of who he is. When we're at our worst, God's love is at its best.

> **God loves us in spite of us, not because of us. He loves us not because of what we do but because of who he is.**

Paul wrote that because of God's grace, you have been "saved." *Saved* is a verb. You can write a verb in past, present, future, or perfect tense.

Past tense speaks of something that has already happened.

Present tense describes something happening right now.

Future tense refers to something that will happen eventually but hasn't yet.

Perfect tense speaks of something that has happened in the past, is still happening in the present, and will continue in the future. It draws attention to the continuing effects of something that has happened in the past.

Paul wrote "saved" in perfect tense! You were saved by God's grace in the past, but the effect is still happening. His grace is always going to impact your life. God will continue giving you new life in your dead places until his work is complete in you.

You never have to feel defeated.

You can never give up.

Because God didn't just save you. He *saves* you. He is constantly saving you.

You can't, but God can. And God will, if you turn to his power.

Exercise 25

Complete these sentences to write out a prayer, being as specific as you can in what you are asking God to do in your life. Use this pattern as many times as you need.

God, I can't:

But you can by:

Principle 25

You can't, but God can.

And God will, if you turn to his power.

But God is so rich in mercy, and he loved us so much, that even though we were dead because of our sins, he gave us life when he raised Christ from the dead. (It is only by God's grace that you have been saved!)

—Ephesians 2:4–5 NLT

5.3 It's All You!

(But Actually Not at All)

I was working out with Paco. (Remember him? Not me, Paco, but him, Paco.) His real name is John. (I told you back in part 1 that I give out nicknames as freely as the Chinese restaurant in the mall food court hands out samples.) One day, we were doing a chest burnout. *Say what?* After lifting several sets of very heavy weights, you switch to low-weight, high-rep bench presses until you are absolutely drained. You then take the weights off the bar and just bench press the bar. If that sounds easy, trust me, it's not after you have just exhausted your chest muscles.

At the end of the workout, the goal was to bench press just the bar fifty times. I did five, then ten. I noticed people were looking at me and laughing. Apparently, seeing a guy who seems to think he's tough bench pressing just the bar—something a middle schooler could do—was funny to these people. But it wasn't to me.

I hit twenty and thought crying was a decent option. I wanted to quit. But Paco wouldn't let me. He shouted encouragement as he stood above me with his legs spread on either side of the bench. (I'm sure that visual only added to the amusement of those watching. A trainer cheering on a guy who is pressing the bar with no weight.)

I got to thirty and hit a wall. I didn't think I could do one more. But Paco was yelling, "C'mon, Paco!" (Remember, we call each other Paco.) "You've got more in you, Paco! Keep going! It's all you!

You can do more!" I kept pushing. I got to forty-five and, now way past crying, thought dying was a better option than continuing.

Paco put his hands under the bar to help lift it up as I pushed. He yelled, "You've got this! You've got more in you! You can do it! It's all you!" The people watching giggled, unimpressed as I strained to bench press a forty-pound bar.

I got to forty-five reps and realized I was done. I knew Paco had the bar, so I took my hands off. To my amazement, the bar kept going up and down. Paco (the other Paco) was lifting and lowering the bar, not recognizing I was no longer involved. As he did my bench presses, all by himself, he yelled, "It's all you! It's all you!" (Paco was really into it.)

When he realized it was not me, at all, it was actually all him, we both burst out laughing.

> **At the end of my power, I discover God's power.**

What I've learned—not at the gym, but in real life—is that at the end of my power, I discover God's power. His power is always there. When I am weak, he is strong.

Willpower doesn't work, but God's power does, and his power is:

- Available
- Accessible
- Active
- Abundant

Let's look at another passage Paul wrote about this dynamic: "So I say, walk by the Spirit, and you will not gratify the desires of the flesh. For the flesh desires what is contrary to the Spirit, and the Spirit what is contrary to the flesh. They are in conflict with each other, so that you are not to do whatever you want" (Gal. 5:16–17).

The "Spirit" is the Holy Spirit; God in us. When you give yourself to God, he gives himself to you. He moves inside of you—like the creme filling in a Twinkie. He lives inside you to empower you to live the life he has for you.

Paul also wrote about the "flesh." The Greek word translated "flesh" is *sarx*, used 149 times in the New Testament.[57] It doesn't mean your skin. Sarx refers to your human nature, your natural self with its weaknesses and sinful desires. That's why "the flesh desires what is contrary to the Spirit." Part of you wants to lead you in a way you really don't want to go; in a way God doesn't want you to go. That part of you explains why you keep doing what you don't want to keep doing, as in:

- "I don't want to keep gambling."
- "I don't want to keep talking about people behind their backs."
- "I don't want to keep looking at that website."
- "I don't want to keep feeling jealous."
- "I don't want to keep spending more money than I have on things I don't even need."
- "I don't want to keep wasting my life scrolling through photos of other people's lives."

I don't want to, but I do.

Why? What is that? That's your flesh. You do what you don't want to do. And then? You swear you won't do it again. And you try, but it doesn't last. Your willpower wilts.

Paul wrote in another letter that we "put no confidence in the flesh" (Phil. 3:3). In other words, we put no confidence in our own willpower.

So what do we put our confidence in? God's power. Paul urges us, "So I say, walk by the Spirit" (Gal. 5:16). Walking by the Spirit, rather than the flesh, is a decision to live, overcome our self-destructive habits, and pursue our goals not in our power but in God's. Because we can't, but he can.

The Greek word translated "walk" is *peripateo*, a present-tense verb. That means you keep doing it; walking by the Spirit is something you can never stop doing, like breathing or preparing for the zombie apocalypse.

Choosing to walk by the Spirit is not a onetime decision or event but an ongoing, habitual way of life. From this moment, and in every moment from now on, I trust in and rely on God's power, not my willpower.

> **Walking by the Spirit is a habitual way of life.**

That sounds great. But how do you really do it? How do you walk by the Spirit?

Let's look at four words that have changed my life and will change yours:

1. Renew
2. Remain
3. Acknowledge
4. Ask

Exercise 26

To illustrate the power of Galatians 5:16–17 in your life, complete the following sentences. Use the pattern as many times as you need.

In my flesh, I constantly struggle with:

But in my spirit, I want to:

Principle 26

**Willpower doesn't work, but God's
power does, and his power is:**

- **Available**
- **Accessible**
- **Active**
- **Abundant**

So I say, walk by the Spirit, and you will not
gratify the desires of the flesh. For the flesh
desires what is contrary to the Spirit, and the Spirit
what is contrary to the flesh. They are in conflict
with each other, so that you are not to do whatever
you want.

—Galatians 5:16–17

5.4 Renew, Remain, Acknowledge, Ask

I told you I'm a world-class nicknamer, right? Then there was the time I learned the entire Napoleon Dynamite dance. As you can tell, I've got a few skills, but handyman around the house is not one of them. I am Mr. Not-So-Handyman.

When Amy and I were first married, we lived in a house built in 1910. (As in the turn of so-not-this-century.) We moved into the house and put our used couch, lamps, and little TV in the den. (For you younger ones, a den is a wannabe living room.)

That night, we tried to turn on a lamp, but the lamp didn't come on. We thought the lamp might have been broken in the move or that the bulb blew out. Then we tried to turn on the TV. It didn't come on either. *Huh?* We tried to turn on the other lamp. Same thing. We realized all the outlets in the den had no power.

I told Amy I'd fix it, that it was probably just one of those fuse thingies. So I pretended like I was "working on" the fuse box. Not wanting to shock myself or blow up the house, I quickly gave up. We bought some extension cords, plugged them into the outlets in the kitchen, ran them through the dining room, and plugged our TV and lamps into those.

The extension cords were an eyesore that we tried to not trip over for *three years*. As we were getting ready to move out of that house, we noticed a light switch on the other side of the wall of the den. *What's this switch?* I flipped it on. Nothing happened. *Why?* I flipped it off. *Wait a second. No, you don't think?* I flipped it back on and walked into the den. I unplugged the lamp from the extension cord and plugged it into the wall. And God said, "Let there be light." Finally the people living in darkness saw a great light, which became a lamp for my feet, a light for my path.

I felt like I should be the star of a new movie, *Dumb and Dumber and Dumbest*. The electricity we'd needed for our den was available the whole time. For three long, extension-cord-dependent, trip-hazardous years. We just didn't know how to access the power.

That is also a fairly good description of my early years of following Jesus. I needed God's power. It was available to me. But I didn't know how to access it. How to live in it. How to walk by the Spirit.

Whoever it is that you want to become or stop being, whatever it is that you want to do or stop doing, you need more than will-power. You need God's power.

God can give you the power to:

- Love someone who is difficult to love
- Serve when you'd rather be served
- Give when it's scary to give
- Study when you'd rather play
- Spend time with your child when you would rather relax

You'll need to go beyond willpower and tap into God's power.

In that decisive moment when you're tempted to buy another pair of shoes online, to worry again, to look again, to gossip again, to drink again, or to call your ex again, how do you rely on God's power—rather than willpower—to overcome the temptation to do wrong?

How do you walk in the Spirit in those moments?

Here are the four words I introduced to you at the end of the last chapter: Renew. Remain. Acknowledge. Ask.

Two for *before* the moment—the *R*'s. Two for *in* the moment—the *A*'s.

Renew

I'm not proud of it. Actually, I'm ashamed of it. In college, my fraternity brothers and I made life all about "getting with girls." That's what we called it back then. For us, "scoring" was success. We mistakenly thought it was how you proved your manhood. I had been living that way for a while and was completely caught up in it.

But then I started seeking God. I felt drawn to Jesus. I was trying to figure out whether the Bible was true. Eventually, I was convinced. I wanted to give my whole life to Jesus. Except I didn't want to give up sex.

Maybe you understand. You might be drawn to Jesus. You want to give your life to him, but there's something you just don't want to give up. Something you don't think you can give up.

Finally, I submitted my life to Jesus. I surrendered. Everything. I told my fraternity brothers I was going to follow Jesus for the rest of my life and that I would not have sex again until I got married. You should have seen the smirks on their faces. They asked one another, "How long is it going to be before Groeschel breaks?" They wondered whether I would last a few weeks or only a couple of days. They made hundred-dollar bets, which was a lot of money for a college student, on how long I'd keep my commitment.

I knew I was in trouble. I knew there was no way I could overcome my flesh and avoid the temptation by willpower. I knew my only chance was God's power. I had to walk in the Spirit. I felt desperate, so I prayed and prayed.

That's when I was led to do something that seemed dramatic but, looking back, was totally necessary. The Holy Spirit led me to stop dating for an extended period. Why was that so crucial, you ask? Because my thinking about women and relationships was a mess. With that wrong thinking, there was no way I could be in a relationship that honored God and the woman I was dating. I needed God to transform my thinking.

He did.

Any of those guys who bet against me lost. They were right about me, but wrong about what God could do in me.

I came out of that season knowing that women were not objects to be used but people to be treasured and respected. God turned my desires for sex (flesh) to desires for purity (Spirit). I was walking by the Spirit. His Spirit.

Today, I am absolutely convinced that the relationship I have with my best friend, Amy, in the intimacy we share and the blessed marriage we enjoy never would have happened had I not surrendered and given God those two years to renew my mind. And, by the way, the personal principles I shared with you in part 3 are how I have trained myself to maintain and grow in what I started in college.

To walk in the Spirit, in God's power, we need to renew our minds: "Therefore, I urge you, brothers and sisters, in view of God's mercy, to offer your bodies as a living sacrifice, holy and pleasing to God—this is your true and proper worship. Do not conform to the pattern of this world, but be transformed by the renewing of your mind. Then you will be able to test and approve what God's will is—his good, pleasing and perfect will" (Rom. 12:1–2).

We are called to live in a way that is holy and pleasing to God. He invites us to be changed, to be different from the rest of the world. The key to living out God's "good, pleasing and perfect will" is being "transformed by the renewing of your mind."

> **When we allow God to change the way we think, it will change how we act.**

When we allow God to change the way we think, it will change how we act, how we respond to opportunities and temptations, how we treat people. It will change everything.

This takes us full circle back to "who before do." You do what you do because of what you think of you. We said that how you think about yourself drives your behavior. Here's another truth bomb: how you think about everything impacts everything.

So we need to renew our minds. We need the truth to be embedded into our thinking. We renew our minds with God's Word so we can start thinking God's thoughts. This is the only way we can be transformed by the renewing of our minds.

You renew your mind by reading the Bible, not a verse or two every week but consistently and voraciously. Just like your succeeding in anything depends on your commitment. (A great resource is to download the YouVersion Bible app and start doing daily Bible plans around topics that interest you or books of the Bible.)

You renew your mind by internalizing Bible verses. As the psalmist wrote, "I have hidden your word in my heart that I might not sin against you" (Ps. 119:11). Pick some verses that speak to:

- Who you want to become
- A sin you want to leave behind
- The habit you want to establish
- The goal you want to accomplish

Write the verses on three-by-five cards and keep them with you, pulling them out and reading them whenever you have some time or when you are tempted or struggling and need to remind yourself of the truth. You can download a Bible memorization app, some of which can make internalizing God's Word easier and almost feel like a fun game.

You also renew your mind by listening to good Bible teaching. Being part of a church where the Bible is taught faithfully is essential. And there's great Bible teaching you can access online.

If you renew your mind—before the moment—you will be ready with God's power in the moment.

Remain

To walk in the Spirit, we need to remain. Jesus said, "Remain in me, and I will remain in you. For a branch cannot produce fruit if it is severed from the vine, and you cannot be fruitful unless you remain in me. Yes, I am the vine; you are the branches. Those who remain in me, and I in them, will produce much fruit. For apart from me you can do nothing" (John 15:4–5 NLT).

He tells us, "Remain in me." When you do, God's power will be unleashed in your life. You will be fruitful. You'll be able to live the life God created you to live.

And notice Jesus also says, "Apart from me you can do nothing." With willpower, you will not be fruitful and will miss out on the life God intends for you.

What did he mean by "remain"?

I want you to play Bible detective for a minute. All of these verses contain the same word we have translated in John 15:4 as "remain"—*meno*. Read through them and see if you can find the one word they all have in common:

- "Mary remained with her about three months, and returned to her house" (Luke 1:56 NKJV).
- "For two whole years Paul stayed there in his own rented house and welcomed all who came to see him" (Acts 28:30).
- "When Jesus stepped ashore, he was met by a demon-possessed man from the town. For a long time this man had not worn clothes or lived in a house, but had lived in the tombs" (Luke 8:27).

- "Stay there, eating and drinking whatever they give you, for the worker deserves his wages. Do not move around from house to house" (Luke 10:7).

You figured it out, right? In each of those verses the word *meno* is associated with the word *house.*

There are other verses where the word *meno* is translated "stay." For instance:

- "They said, 'Rabbi' (which means 'Teacher'), 'where are you staying?'" (John 1:38).
- "Peter stayed in Joppa for some time with a tanner named Simon" (Acts 9:43).
- "Erastus stayed in Corinth, and I left Trophimus sick in Miletus" (2 Tim. 4:20).

So what is Jesus inviting us to do? To make him our home and stay in him.

Jesus says, "Remain in me" and adds, "as I also remain in you" (John 15:4). Jesus is making you an offer. "Live inside of me, and let me live inside of you."

He's talking about a closeness, an intimacy, that comes:

- Through *prayer,* where you regularly pour out your heart to God, and it's real and raw and authentic and vulnerable
- Through *being silent and enjoying his presence,* where you get quiet before God and just know him in a relationship
- Through *saying yes to him,* where you do whatever he's asking and live in obedience. "Jesus replied, 'Anyone who loves me will obey my teaching. My Father will love them, and we will come to them and make our home with them'" (John 14:23).

If you remain in Jesus—before the moment—you will be ready with God's power in the moment.

How do you walk by the Spirit so in that moment of opportunity or temptation, you're plugged into God's power?

Two *R* words need to happen before the moment: renew and remain.

Two *A* words need to happen in the moment: acknowledge and ask.

Acknowledge

The moment will come. You will have an opportunity to do something you want to do, maybe the habit you've decided to start, but it won't be easy. Or you will be tempted to do something you don't want to do, perhaps the habit you've decided to stop, and it would be so easy.

In that moment, you will hear a voice.

Not an audible voice, but you'll hear it. Yours may not sound like Paco when I'm lifting weights, but mine does. The voice will be cheering you on. "You got this. You can do it! It's all you!"

But you have to ignore that voice.

That voice is coming from your flesh. It's the natural, human part of you that thinks it's got the strength of Dwayne "The Rock" Johnson plus John Cena times three hundred—plus steroids.

Your flesh is overly confident, dangerously prideful, and cannot be trusted.

Ignore that voice and acknowledge that you don't have the power you need. Say, with Paul, "I want to do what is right, but I can't" (Rom. 7:18 NLT) and with Jesus, "Apart from Jesus, I can do nothing" (personalizing John 15:5).

The Twelve Steps, which have been so successful in getting people unstuck, begin with Step One, "We admitted we were powerless over sin—that our lives had become unmanageable." Then Step Two, "We came to believe that a Power greater than ourselves could restore us to sanity."[58] If you go to a Twelve Step meeting, hoping to finally find freedom, you'll be taught you have to acknowledge you can't, but God can.

I get that. In my battle with alcohol back in my college years, I kept deciding to quit and believing that voice that told me, "You got this. You can do it! It's all you!" I'd be like, *Yeah, that voice knows how awesome I am! I got this. I can do anything I put my mind to. If I can conceive it, I can achieve it!* Then I'd realize I had a beer in my hand. It was painful and embarrassing to admit I did not have what it took to quit. I couldn't do what I needed to do.

But then I could. I quit drinking.

I could when I admitted I couldn't. I had what it took when I could no longer deny that I did not have what it took.

The same was true when I decided the way to transform my mind about the opposite sex was to distance myself from females and give God the next two years. I remained in Jesus—before the moment—so I could be ready with God's power in the moment.

Acknowledging "I can't" is the path to possessing a power you don't possess. What you need is the God of resurrection working on your behalf, walking with you, his power coursing through your veins, releasing you from what's held you back for so long.

> **Acknowledging "I can't" is the path to possessing a power you don't possess.**

Ask

You've tried and tried. You've done everything you can, but you always end up back in the same place. Like the lady in the news story, you're still stuck on that toilet. You may feel like giving up because it's obvious you don't have what it takes.

If so, you are at a critical moment.

This is your chance. Because instead of giving up, you can look up. Look up and find a God who loves you, has what you need, and is just waiting for you to ask.

When my son Stephen was sixteen, he came to me very nervously. He started talking, but I was having a little trouble putting all of his words together. I definitely caught the word *protein*, and he mentioned at least twice that he knew I was really busy. I finally told him to just say what he wanted.

He steadied himself and asked, "Dad, I've been wanting to work out. I'm wondering if I could work out with you so you can show me some techniques on lifting weights?" Yes! I was filled with joy. I had been waiting, hoping he might ask that exact question. I loved working out, loved my son even more, and loved the idea of sharing my knowledge and time with him. I couldn't believe he was nervous to ask me for something I wanted so badly to give him.

God is a good Father who loves you, has what you need, and is just waiting for you to ask.

So ask. Just like Stephen did with me.

In James 4, we read about the "desires that battle within you" (v. 1). James writes, "You desire but do not have. . . . You cannot get what you want" (v. 2). What is the real problem? James continues, "You do not have because you do not ask God" (v. 2). So ask. James chapter one says, "You should ask God, who gives generously to all without finding fault, and it will be given to you" (v. 5).

Amazing, right? You might feel nervous or embarrassed to ask God for his power, or to ask God for anything, because of your weakness and sin. But remember that he is a God of grace. He loves you unconditionally. God is generous. He loves to give. He does so without finding fault.

He wants to give you his power, and when you are "in the moment," his power is what you need.

So acknowledge, "God, I know I can't. I don't have the power. I can't do this," and then ask, "God, I know you can. You have the power. Please give me the power I need in this moment." Then move forward in confidence, knowing God gives generously and will provide all the power you need and more.

Asking God to strengthen you in that moment is crucial. But to walk in the Spirit, we need to ask all the time. It should be the undercurrent of our day, all day, every day. So if someone followed you around and kept asking you questions about what's going on inside your mind and heart, you would sound like a broken record.

What are you doing? "I'm waking up and asking the Spirit to lead me through my day."

What are you doing now? "I'm asking the Spirit to keep me spiritually strong today."

And what are you doing now? "I'm asking the Spirit to give me the right words to say to this person."

"I'm asking the Spirit to help me keep my mouth shut right now."

"I'm asking the Spirit to give me the power to say yes to what I know is right."

"I'm asking the Spirit to give me the power to say no to what I know is wrong."

"I'm asking the Spirit to help me show love to this person."

You have a Father God who loves you and loves to give good gifts to his children. Just ask. Ask God to give you his power. To help you do what you need to do. Trust that he loves you, loves to help you, and would love to make his power available to you.

If you do that, if you renew and remain before the moment, if you acknowledge and ask in the moment, you will find you have flipped the switch and now have power you didn't before.

You're walking by the Spirit.

You're taking steps—not in your power but in God's power.

Exercise 27

Use the four keywords in this chapter as a guide for prayer, and complete these sentences.

Father, I pray today you would renew *my mind by helping me to:*

Father, help me to remain *in you today as/when I:*

Father, today I acknowledge *my weakness and your power. I know I am weak, but you are strong, in:*

*Father, today, I recognize your great love for me and how you desire to give me good gifts, so I **ask** you to:*

Principle 27

If you renew and remain before the moment, and if you acknowledge and ask in the moment, you will have God's power to walk by the Spirit.

Remain in me, and I will remain in you. For a branch cannot produce fruit if it is severed from the vine, and you cannot be fruitful unless you remain in me.

Yes, I am the vine; you are the branches. Those who remain in me, and I in them, will produce much fruit. For apart from me you can do nothing.

—John 15:4–5 NLT

5.5 Steps

We walk by the Spirit. Or as other translations word it, we "keep in step with the Spirit." I love the idea of a step, of taking a step.

I remember when my kids were babies. After months of crawling around, they would start pulling themselves up on the couch. At first, they would very cautiously balance on their little feet. Eventually, they would get the feel for standing upright. As a dad, I thought that was when the fun started. I watched, smiling, as they put both arms straight forward and tentatively put one foot out like baby Frankensteins. As their father, I cheered as they took those first steps.

As you start to walk by the Spirit, it might feel awkward, like a baby taking first steps. You're moving forward into new habits, learning to rely on God's power instead of willpower. It may be new to you. It might be intimidating. That's okay. We all have to start somewhere.

It's actually exciting. You're getting to venture out on a new journey. You are going to need God and experience him in a way you never have before. Your new direction will be scary, but exhilarating.

I have to believe that your taking those first steps is when the fun starts for God. He created you to walk with him, and you're doing it!

As you do, picture God cheering you on. He is excited for you. He is grateful for the opportunity to be in a deeper partnership with you than you may have allowed in the past. He is rooting for you.

So do it. Take a step. Don't put off another day living the life God has in mind for you. Don't just sit there and say, "Maybe tomorrow." Today is the day. Take a step with the Holy Spirit. Then take another step. Then another.

It might sound impossible right now, but remember, this is who you are. Your true identity is as a child of God. God made you to love you. You were created to live hand in hand with him. You were designed to follow him in a faith-fueled, sometimes risky adventure. Taking these steps might feel unnatural now, but there is nothing more natural to who you truly are.

So take a step. Then another step. Then another. Those steps will go from unusual to habitual. You will be walking in the Spirit of God. And remember, when you walk in the Spirit of God "you will not gratify the desires of the flesh" (Gal. 5:16).

As you walk, will you trip up and maybe even fall down? Of course, you will. Which is not the answer you want! We all want to be flawless, but only Jesus lived a perfect life. As you take steps, you will trip. So what should you do when you fall? Get back up and keep walking. You're new at this. Falling isn't failure. You're learning and growing.

It's like my daughter learning to walk. Imagine her getting up on two legs and taking her first wobbly step. Everyone in the room cheers wildly. "She's walking!" If she takes another step, then falls, no one's going to say, "Oh. This baby can't walk. She failed. What a loser." No. When that happens, you help the baby get up. You give the baby a hug. You help the baby get back on her feet. Then she takes another step.

Paul urged us to keep walking in the Spirit, not in our own power but in God's power. If you fall down, get back up. Keep walking in the Spirit.

That's winning, and there is no such thing as losing. You're in this for the long haul. Right? Remember, it's about progress, not perfection. So when you're winning, you're winning. When you're losing, you're learning.

When you're winning, you're winning. When you're losing, you're learning.

Just keep moving forward.

As you continue walking, you'll find that you are moving out of your past and into your future.

Let me warn you: this won't happen overnight.

- You are walking into your future, into the who you want to be.
- You are walking away from the sin or self-destructive behavior you want to leave behind.
- You are walking toward the new habits and new life you've wanted for so long.

You are walking, not running. Paul did not say we run with the Spirit. We walk in the Spirit.

That's one of the obstacles we'll face as we do this. As we've learned, it takes time to get to what you want most. What you want now almost always has an immediate payoff.

That cookie tastes good now.

Sexual sin feels good now.

Sending that mean text when you are angry feels great now.

Buying the new car, even though you can't afford it, feels awesome now.

The desires of the flesh have an immediate payoff. But what you want most almost always takes time.

What do you want most?

A godly marriage?

To be closer to God?

A rich spiritual legacy?

Financial freedom?

A meaningful ministry?

You can have it! But not now. You walk there, with the Spirit, while depending on God, moment by moment. It will take time, but it will be worth it. You may miss out on some short-term fleeting satisfaction, but you will realize you chose the greater reward. You chose what you want most over what you want now.

You can get there. You can enjoy the life you dream about but have not yet experienced.

You can get unstuck.

You. You who could never do it before.

You. You'll be doing it!

But it won't be you.

It will be God. Through you.

You can change!

Your life can be transformed.

You can't. But he can.

Exercise 28

Taking into account everything you have learned throughout the book, and all that God has shown you as you've worked through every exercise, let's calculate your next steps.

I know the first step I need to take in starting a new habit is:

I know the first step I need to take in stopping an old habit is:

The one change I believe God is calling me to make—in his power, not my own—is:

Principle 28

When you're winning, you're winning.
When you're losing, you're learning.

And now, just as you accepted Christ Jesus as your Lord, you must continue to follow him. Let your roots grow down into him, and let your lives be built on him. Then your faith will grow strong in the truth you were taught, and you will overflow with thankfulness.

—Colossians 2:6–7 NLT

Acknowledgments

I'd like to express my deepest gratitude to all my friends who helped make this book possible.

Amy Groeschel, thank you for your constant encouragement! You are my favorite thing about everything. I love you with all my heart.

Vince Antonucci, you make writing a blast! You are truly one of the brightest and most gifted people I've ever known. Thank you for pouring your heart into this project with me. I'm thankful to have you as a writing partner and a friend.

Robert Nolan, thank you for adding the finishing touches. You made such a difference on this book as well as *Winning the War in Your Mind*.

Tom Winters, thanks for your years of friendship and partnership on books!

Webster Younce, Andy Rogers, Brian Phipps, Curt Diepenhorst, Sara Colley, Paul Fisher, Katie Painter, Sarah Falter, and the whole team at Zondervan, I love your heart to impact lives with the written word. You honor Jesus with the work you do, and it shows.

Adrianne Manning, Jenn McCarty, Courtney Donald, and Katherine Fedor, y'all are the best. Thank you for all your behind-the-scenes help! (And thanks for tolerating my zigs and zags.) You are a gift to our ministry!

To the reader, thank you for believing you can change. I am praying God uses this book to help shape you to exactly who he wants you to become.

Appendix

Identity Statements and Bible Verses

- Sought after (Isa. 62:12)
- Precious in his sight (Isa. 43:4)
- A new creation in Christ (2 Cor. 5:17)
- Not condemned (Rom. 8:1)
- Forgiven (Col. 1:14)
- Loved (1 John 3:1)
- Accepted (Rom. 15:7)
- A child of God (John 1:12)
- Jesus' friend (John 15:14)
- Free (John 8:36)
- The temple of God (1 Cor. 6:19)
- God's treasured possession (Deut. 7:6)
- Complete in Christ (Col. 2:10 NLT)
- Chosen (Col. 3:12)
- Called (2 Tim. 1:9)
- An ambassador of the Most High God (2 Cor. 5:20)
- God's masterpiece (Eph. 2:10 NLT)
- Able to do all things through Christ, who gives you strength (Phil. 4:13)
- More than a conqueror through Jesus, who loves you (Rom. 8:37)

Notes

1. James G. March, "Rule Following," chap. 2 in *A Primer on Decision Making: How Decisions Happen* (New York: Free Press, 1994).
2. Yes, I am aware of how close a line I'm walking to this becoming a Dr. Seuss book. *We can't put who before do, but we do. Do you? Who you are is why you do what you do. One you, two you, which you is the true you?*
3. James Clear, *Atomic Habits: An Easy and Proven Way to Build Good Habits and Break Bad Ones* (New York: Penguin Random House, 2018), 33.
4. If you want to understand cybernetics theory, ask someone other than me. It has to do with studying circular, causal chains and their relationship with actions taken toward a desired goal. The concepts are beyond the education I received at Oklahoma City University and Phillips Theological Seminary. Mark Batterson explains cybernetics theory in his book *Win the Day: Seven Daily Habits to Help You Stress Less and Accomplish More* (Colorado Springs: Multnomah, 2020), 12.
5. Charlotte Nickerson, "Looking-Glass Self: Theory, Definition and Examples," *Simply Psychology*, November 10, 2021, www .simplypsychology.org/charles-cooleys-looking-glass-self.html.
6. Here's a video of the speech: Matthew McConaughey, "Academy Awards Acceptance Speech" (86th Academy Awards, Dolby Theatre, Los Angeles, CA, March 2, 2014), www.youtube.com /watch?v=wD2cVhC-63I.
7. Hal Hershfield, "The Psychology of Your Future Self," YouTube, July 11, 2021, www.youtube.com/watch?v=QBdIeC7FYkU.
8. Benjamin Hardy, "Take Ownership of Your Future Self," *Harvard Business Review*, August 28, 2020, hbr.org/2020/08/take -ownership-of-your-future-self.
9. Dan Gilbert, "The Psychology of Your Future Self" (TED2014, Vancouver, Canada, March 18, 2014), 2:40, www.ted.com/talks /dan_gilbert_the_psychology_of_your_future_self.

10. Carol S. Dweck, *Mindset: The New Psychology of Success* (New York: Random House, 2006). And here's a TED Talk she gave: www.youtube.com/watch?v=hiiEeMN7vbQ.

11. Mauro Prosperi, "How I Drank Urine and Bat Blood to Survive," BBC News, November 27, 2014, www.bbc.com/news/magazine -30046426.

12. "Do Written Goals Really Make a Difference?" UGM Consulting, January 20, 2021, ugmconsulting.com/do-written-goals-really -make-a-difference.

13. John Newton, "Amazing Grace! (How Sweet the Sound)," 1779, in *Ancient and Modern* (London: Hymns Ancient and Modern, 2013), no. 587, on Hymnary.org, hymnary.org/text/amazing_grace _how_sweet_the_sound.

14. Jessica Dickler, "As Inflation Heats Up, 64% of Americans Are Now Living Paycheck to Paycheck," CNBC.com, March 8, 2022, www.cnbc.com/2022/03/08/as-prices-rise-64-percent-of -americans-live-paycheck-to-paycheck.html; Andrew Herrig, "Personal Finance Statistics 2021: Shocking Facts on Money, Debt, and More," Wealthy Nickel, January 9, 2021, wealthynickel .com/personal-finance-statistics; Erin El Issa, "2021 American Household Credit Card Debt Study," NerdWallet, January 11, 2022, www.nerdwallet.com/blog/average-credit-card-debt-household.

15. Jerry M. Hullinger, "1 Corinthians 9:24 Commentary," Precept Austin, updated April 15, 2021, www.preceptaustin.org /1_corinthians_924_commentary.

16. Ibid.

17. *Star Wars: The Empire Strikes Back*, directed by Irvin Kershner, written by George Lucas (San Francisco: Lucasfilm, 1980), www.youtube.com/watch?v=eExL1VLkQYk.

18. The drawstring is technically called a "belt." I highly recommend you not say "drawstring" in front of people with higher-ranking belts. At least not while you are within their reach. (But it sure looked like a drawstring!)

19. Quoted in John Maxwell, *How to Lead When Your Boss Can't (or Won't)* (New York: HarperCollins, 2019), 114.

20. "Losing Weight," Centers for Disease Control and Prevention, last

reviewed September 19, 2022, www.cdc.gov/healthyweight
/losing_weight/index.html.

21. James Clear, "Avoid the Second Mistake," James Clear (website), accessed October 6, 2022, jamesclear.com/second-mistake.

22. Adults may be promoted through belts: white, blue, purple, brown, and black. Each belt has five levels, a clear belt and then four stripes that may be awarded for time, knowledge, behavior, and tournament performance. Learn more on the North American Brazilian Jiu-Jitsu Federation website: www.nabjjf.com/index .php/belt-system.

23. Hold up. Before we move on, are we not going to acknowledge this sentence? "My hunch is you don't deviate much on what you munch for lunch"? Are you kidding me? The greatest writer of all time, Shakespeare, wrote lines like, "Men at some time are masters of their fates. / The fault, dear Brutus, is not in our stars, / But in ourselves" (*Julius Caesar*, 1.2.139–41). Yeah, well, I rhymed hunch, munch, and lunch. Take that, William!

24. David T. Neal, Wendy Wood, and Jeffrey M. Quinn, "Habits— A Repeat Performance," *Current Directions in Psychological Science* 15, no. 4 (August 2006): doi.org/10.1111/j.1467-8721 .2006.00435.x.

25. Will Durant, *The Story of Philosophy* (New York: Simon and Schuster, 1926), 87.

26. Charles Duhigg, *The Power of Habit: Why We Do What We Do in Life and Business* (New York: Random House, 2014).

27. Clear, *Atomic Habits*, 50.

28. Here is a more scientific explanation: Your brain makes a neurotransmitter called dopamine. Dopamine is like a brain cookie. A dopamine release makes you feel good. Dopamine is released when your brain expects a reward or is experiencing a pleasurable situation. Drugs release dopamine. That's why drugs can be addictive. Sex releases dopamine. That's why sex can be addictive. Food releases dopamine. That's why food can be addictive. You get it.

29. Nicholas A. Christakis and James H. Fowler, "The Spread of Obesity in a Large Social Network over Thirty-Two Years," *New England Journal of Medicine*, July 26, 2007, doi.org/10.1056 /NEJMsa066082.

30. Chip Heath and Dan Heath, *Switch: How to Change Things When Change Is Hard* (New York: Broadway, 2010), 192–93.

31. Clear, *Atomic Habits*, 84.

32. Sarah Milne, Sheina Orbell, and Paschal Sheeran, "Combining Motivational and Volitional Interventions to Promote Exercise Participation: Protection Motivation Theory and Implementation Intentions," *British Journal of Health Psychology* 7, no. 2 (May 2002): doi.org/10.1348/135910702169420.

33. Pretty sure I just made that word up.

34. James Clear, "How the Two-Minute Rule Can Help You Beat Procrastination and Start New Habits," CNBC.com, February 1, 2019, www.cnbc.com/2019/02/01/the-2-minute-rule-how-to-stop-procrastinating-and-start-new-habits.html.

35. You know, like LarryBoy from *VeggieTales*.

36. Jim Collins, *Good to Great* (New York: HarperCollins, 2001), 14.

37. Ibid., 92.

38. Malcolm Gladwell, "The 10,000-Hour Rule," chap. 2 in *Outliers: The Story of Success* (New York: Little, Brown and Company, 2008).

39. If not, google "OBJ catch," and behold the greatness.

40. Gladwell, *Outliers*.

41. Ryan Ward, "Lakers Legend Kobe Bryant Never Got Bored with the Basics," Lakers Nation, February 14, 2017, lakersnation.com/lakers-legend-kobe-bryant-never-got-bored-with-the-basics/2017/02/14.

42. "Kobe Bryant's Mamba Mentality," Nike News, August 23, 2020, news.nike.com/news/kobe-bryant-nike-believe-film.

43. This catchphrase was made famous by Sonny the Cuckoo Bird, a legendary comedic TV actor in the 1980s and '90s. Sonny now lives a quiet life in the Hollywood Hills, though he's still reportedly prone to sudden outbursts over breakfast.

44. Gretchen Rubin, "Stop Expecting to Change Your Habit in Twenty-One Days," *Psychology Today*, October 21, 2009, www.psychologytoday.com/us/blog/the-happiness-project/200910/stop-expecting-change-your-habit-in-21-days.

45. Unless the month is February. But we're going to ignore February. It kills the illustration.

46. Jim Schleckser, "Why Einstein Considered Compound Interest the Most Powerful Force in the Universe," Inc., www.inc.com/jim

-schleckser/why-einstein-considered-compound-interest-most
-powerful-force-in-universe.html.

47. Anthony Robbins, special message about *The Compound Effect*, by
    Darren Hardy (New York: Vanguard Press, 2010).

48. Clear, *Atomic Habits*, 18.

49. Billy Graham, "Guideposts Classics: Prayer Tips from Billy
    Graham," *Guideposts*, August 1960, www.guideposts.org/inspiration
    /inspiring-stories/stories-of-faith/guideposts-classics-prayer-tips
    -from-billy-graham.

50. C. S. Lewis, *Mere Christianity* (New York: HarperOne, 2001), 132.

51. Richard Carlson, *Don't Sweat the Small Stuff . . . and It's All Small
    Stuff: Simple Ways to Keep the Little Things from Taking Over Your
    Life* (New York: Hyperion, 1997).

52. Clear, "Figure 2" in *Atomic Habits*, 22.

53. Ibid.

54. Roxana Hegeman, "Sheriff: Woman Sat on Boyfriend's Toilet for
    Two Years," *Wichita Eagle*, August 25, 2014, www. kansas.com
    /news/local/article1011284.html.

55. Vince Antonucci, *Restore: Break Out of Your Past and Into God's
    Future* (Carol Stream, IL: Tyndale, 2018), 56–57.

56. Roy F. Baumeister et al., "Ego Depletion: Is the Active Self a Limited
    Resource?" *Journal of Personality and Social Psychology* 74, no. 5
    (1998): doi.org/10.1037/0022-3514.74.5.1252; Hans Villarica, "The
    Chocolate-and-Radish Experiment That Birthed the Modern
    Conception of Willpower," *Atlantic*, April 9, 2012, www.theatlantic
    .com/health/archive/2012/04/the-chocolate-and-radish-experiment
    -that-birthed-the-modern-conception-of-willpower/255544.

57. Bible Hub, biblehub.com/greek/strongs_4561.htm.

58. "The Twelve Steps," Alcoholics Anonymous, www.aa.org/the
    -twelve-steps.

Personal.
Practical.
Powerful.

CRAIG GROESCHEL
LEADERSHIP PODCAST

Subscribe to the **Craig Groeschel Leadership Podcast** on Apple Podcasts or wherever you listen to podcasts.

Visit **www.llfe.church/leadershippodcast** to find the episode videos, leader guides, discussion questions, and more.

 Apple Podcasts   **Spotify**

 **Google Podcasts**   **YouTube**